Constellations at Twilight

Val J. Littman

Constellations at Twilight

ISBN: Softcover 978-1-951472-66-5

Copyright © 2020 by Val J. Littman

All rights reserved. No part of this book may be reproduced or transmitted in any form or by any means, electronic or mechanical, including photocopying, recording, or by any information storage and retrieval system, without permission in writing from the publisher.

www.parsonsporch.com

The author has researched the quotations in this book through individual online research and through Publisher Licensing Service. If a copyright holder sees a failing to give proper credit or the use is not permitted under Fair Use practices, please contact the author at vallittman@gmail.com to discuss future corrections.

Dedication

I wish to dedicate this work to my nephews and their families, the grand-nieces, and grand-nephews. For the early-life parts of this story they were, not yet, even a twinkle in their fathers' eyes. Perhaps the story will be interesting to them, perhaps instructive, perhaps it will help them to know their roots. Perhaps it will help them reach for the stars.

Whether we live to an old age, die young, whether we are sick or infirmed, rich or poor; such matters are often beyond our control. But the integrity with which we live our life; how we treat others. our thoughts and actions, these are truly ours and who we are.

Table of Contents

Preface – Why this Book and this Title...7
Earliest Memories 12
Days of Childhood — Age Six to the "Tweens"...................................21
Diocesan Preparatory Seminary Days 42
College Years at Prep Sem – a Brief Interlude.....................................54
Saint John Vianney Seminary Years[1] 57
New Haven 68
Our Lady of Victory Basilica..75
Beginning Again, Chicago 87
Chicago, Love and Care Years [1] 96
An Epilogue..110
Annotated Bibliography..113

Preface – Why this Book and this Title

After writing my first book, *Bright Sun & Long Shadows* and the second, *Le Petit Jardin de L'âme*, it seemed logical to continue a chronological saga of life in retirement. But while I have kept the practice of correspondence to friends and family which formed the general outline of previous books, I found my energies drawn to the other end of the life-spectrum rather than continuing in chronological fashion about our life in Panama — I was drawn to the beginnings.

Many times, in the comfort of our retirement in Panama I found myself drifting to memories of earlier, formative life-experiences. It was not unusual in my septuagenarian years for me to reflect on how moments from my personal history shape my present-day relationships and events. For better or worse there is a link of my present to earlier times. Sometimes there is a twinkle of the past reflected in my present reaction, or perhaps a bit of guidance by learning from personal history.

There was also an increased awareness that as our friendships in this current chapter of retirement grew, they also diversified. Social networks were no longer as clearly determined by common bonds to others in our professional circle. In these retirement years I grew to discover that I (or together, Linda and I) had made life-choices much different than many of our current friends and acquaintances around us. Those differences were sometimes highlighted by our friends' comments, sometimes I silently recognized the differences internally and sometimes an insight arose in a small group; a dialogue group formed by Linda based on a methodology of David Bohm.[1]

As an example of this diversity in retirement let me just elaborate on one variable. During most of my work-life the people with whom I spent my time were "like me" in that there was some common educational background in liberal arts, and the social sciences, and in ministry or other helping professions. Although I prided myself in developing a diverse group of friends, and our Chicago-based professional lives was as varied as urban life would be, there was a certain self-selection process among the people with whom I worked and spent more than one-third of each day. I found that in retirement much of that commonality thinned out. As work-life friends retire, they migrate to different communities. In retirement we found ourselves in a new group with perhaps a different commonality

We found in retirement to Panama, even more so than in our first retirement to France, that the largest common denominator was international living, and secondarily the choice of the rainforest beauty of Altos del Maria. I can safely say that during my work-life neither of these variables was a primary driver in the development of personal relationships. And so, we are surrounded in retirement by a diverse group of people with few things in common other than the place where we live. For instance, in my work-life I knew not one person whose military career joined them to me in my circle of friends, or information technology was at best a sideline of a few acquaintances. Physicists, and engineers were few and far between in my earlier life. It was doctors and medical professionals, lawyers, social workers, psychologists, psychiatrists, professors, and clergy that formed most of my social circle. In retirement, I have neighbors and friends who chose the military as a career, tech savvy computer specialists, and many who have created their own successful businesses in workplace worlds far away from the entrepreneurs, in the fields of psychotherapy and organizational consulting that I knew in Chicago. And there were many new acquaintances who retired from multiple careers. These people all have their own life lessons to share; often from different life journeys, offering different perspectives than my own. This transition to international retirement living could be summarized in the following way: In my work life, my contribution may have been unique, but more like a nuanced variation as one among many around me, who had much in common. In this chapter of international retirement living I found that we all came at a common experience, problem, or conversation topic, from vastly diverse backgrounds often with little in common but the present day.

At times I realize that some of my life journey was unique to me and at other times I saw that my experiences in life were a part of a larger common journey of humanity. In one way or another we had the common yet varied experience of just growing up. But then there are those different life experiences that are specialized or selective based on who I was, how I was educated, the family in which I grew up and the social network in which I lived and worked that formed me in a different way than my neighbors.

Life journeys are seen through lenses and facets uniquely cut and shaped, that now shed light on the present in unexpected ways. In many ways my past determines how I see the present and the future. And this is highlighted in my retirement years because of the diversity of the community and friendships made.

I began to see that glimmers of childhood whimsy, innocence, awe and fear, the curiosities of teen-years searching a horizon well beyond my comprehension, and the explorations, challenges and successes of my early adult life, provided present-day direction for me like constellations in the sky at twilight. As if some far away patterns of light were offering direction or, in some cases, were affecting,[2] not only how I saw the present but that I see things that some others do not.

The image of stars as depicted in Antoine de Saint-Exupéry in *Le Petit Prince*, came to mind.

Right before the little prince departs from the earth, the Little Prince makes this idea more explicit:

"All men have stars," [the prince said.] "but they are not the same things for different people. For some, who are travelers, the stars are guides. For others they are no more than little lights in the sky. For others, who are scholars, they are problems. For my businessman they were wealth. But all these stars are silent.

You—you alone—will have the stars as no one else has them."

To the naked eye, stars are a barely visible series of points of light in the sky. Yet, from ancient times, human ingenuity, in a quest for meaning and direction, has seen some relationship of time and space in a galaxy far-far-away and our life here-and-now.

I should say that I am neither an astronomer nor an astrologer and have no more than a passing curiosity about my astrological sign. I am more drawn to references to constellations in Holy Books; Biblical literature (Genesis, Job, The Psalms, Acts, I-Corinthians, and Revelation); The Quran (Surat Al-Ḥijr), and an abundance of references in classical literature. I am drawn to the symbolic and metaphorical imagery where we have made some connection of these points of light and our present day.

My experiences, like life-constellations, form a way in my evening of life, to understand not only how I arrived at this present but how I see a way to the future; be it the near-future of the next day or a more distant future beyond my personal horizon. In this way *Constellations at Twilight* is not simply a telling of childhood memories but how these remembered experiences serve as a connection of these past points of life to where I am today and for the days ahead or in a future beyond what I can envision. Surely, the images in *Constellations at Twilight* are drawn from my chronological life and relationships but they have become Eidetic Images;[3] not merely vivid but effective in shaping my present and a guide to the future.

Gentle Reader, it is true that much of what you will read happened in a land long ago and far away but the imprint those experiences, along with my journeys in education, in theology and psychology and personal spirituality have stitched together, a present day reality which sheds light upon and directs my life in the now. Such *Constellations at Twilight* have been a guide for me in present day conversations, decisions, and contributions to our life in retirement. And perhaps they will encourage you, to search your own horizon for points of enlightenment based on your life-journey.

"You live through that little piece of time that is yours, but that piece of time is not only your own life, it is the summing-up of all the other lives that are simultaneous with yours ....What you are is an expression of History"
— Robert Penn Warren, *"World Enough and Time"*

And so, I put my life out there for whatever benefit it may be to others. Perhaps, because of reading this book, others will be encouraged to discover their points of light, searching their night-sky of long ago, to see more clearly their way in this present day. Perhaps, my own life-events will help to broaden the range of normal for them to find a place in a grand and varied universe. Perhaps *Constellations at Twilight* can lead to a celebration that you have found not only your way through the maze of your life experience but parts of it continue to guide you now; looking at life experiences much as one would look into the night sky for direction into your tomorrow.

Twilight, it should be noted, happens for us twice in each 24-hour period; at the end of our daylight before the night and again at the first hints of a new day. Just as Twilight occurs at Sunset and Sunrise the events from points of my early life form Constellations to guide me in my twilight years and perhaps into some more distant and timeless tomorrow.

The beginnings of this book will be somewhat of a departure from the chronological memoire of retirement years. Yes, I hope to write a book that begins "at the beginning" as best I can remember. But there will be a back-and-forth between recalling early life events and their link to my present-day understanding. Early memories and perhaps early life-lessons created images and allegories which live on into adult life and old age.

Some of this approach has been stimulated by the realization in past few years that I am now "the old man" of the Littman family. My father's death at the age of 80 (April 07, 2008), my brother's early death at age 60 (November 04, 2009), the celebration of my mother's 90th birthday in 02 May 2017 and her death (November 08 of 2018) make me the sole survivor of my nuclear family. There is no one left who remembers me from the beginning. So, there is a part of me that chose to write this memoire as a reflection, as a way to pass on to the next generation, my nephews, and grand-nieces and grand-nephews and those friends beyond family, what I have cherished. While I have known for a long time that I would not have biological heirs, there remains the belief that every life has some legacy. And writing and publishing is my way to pass on to others life-time lessons.

For those who wish it, *Constellations at Twilight* can be received as a gift given to inspire you, to look back and look beyond life-experiences to light your way like constellations at twilight. Or perhaps it is just a good read, enjoy. A story well told holds opens new horizons for those who can hear it.

Preface Notes:

[1] Bohm Dialogue is a form of communication within a group in which participants attempt to reach a common understanding, experiencing everyone's point of view fully, equally, and nonjudgmentally. This can lead to new and deeper understanding for the individuals. The purpose is to solve the communication crises that face society, and indeed the whole of human nature and consciousness. Group members apply a theoretical understanding of the way thoughts relate to universal reality. It is named after physicist **David Bohm** who originally proposed this form of dialogue. (adapted by the author from Wikipedia)

[2] I use *effecting* here deliberately – and I hope correctly. Whereas the expected use would be *affecting* – meaning to influence or impact. However, I mean *effect* – to produce or to cause to come into being. I believe that present choices have a cause/effect relationship. Some past experiences, much as a specific facet, cut into the diamond, effects the brilliance of the diamond in a unique way. The same diamond, cut differently, reflects the same light differently.

[3] In the mid 1980's as part of personal growth and development of my private practice in psychotherapy, I became acquainted with the use of Eidetic Imagery – notably in the work of Akhter Ahsen and Richard Olney (Dick Olney 1914-1994, Self-Acceptance Training) Eidetic imagery and Self-Acceptance Training provided a way for me personally, and eventually through me for my clients, to experience myself/their self in a given moment without the inhibition of self-criticism, self-judgment, or self-evaluation. Distinct from self-esteem this approach provided a path of remembering and re-experiencing our greater, essential self. An **eidetic image** is a type of vivid mental image, that effects our present. Eidetic images may, or may not, be derived from an actual external event or memory. It was identified in the early twentieth century as a distinct phenomenon by psychologists including E.R. Jaensch, Heinrich Klüver, Gordon Allport and Frederic Bartlett.

Earliest Memories

As I begin, I realize that there are memories that have involved and enveloped me from my first-hand experience and then there are "memories" which have been handed down to me. Most of the experiences in this book are firsthand experiences, although it should be noted there are "second-hand memories" that are handed down to us that also influence who we become.

It is important to discern the difference; is this my memory of my experience or is this a memory given to me by someone else. Here's an example. There have been times where shoeboxes filled with old photos came out of the closet and were shared, usually with a bit of storytelling involved. The photos prompted a narrative that was simply too early for me to actually have a memory of the event, based on the normal developmental curve for early childhood memories. And there were others where I had some vague memory but the family story may be much more vivid or perhaps even very different from that which I remembered. And although not included in the shoe-box of photos there is the possibility that one could have an undeveloped memory; one based on actual first-hand experience but the link to a specific event is a bit fuzzy – a primitive "hunch" or visceral reaction without a historic connection to a specific event. In this last case scenario, the event may have been repressed or in some cases simply occurred very early in the child's development and is fleshed out or validated later by subsequent events.

Sometimes in my life, family recollections, most often from my mother, found validation in some different event which was a part of my memory. Some events have two (or more) memories, or converge from two (or more) sources; an event, one not remembered by me but recalled by my mother, and the same or similar event but which was a part of my personal memory that had the same or similar significance. Where this congruence occurred, it seemed that one validated the other experience.

An example: through the years my mother told the story, usually around my birthday, of how proud my father was when I was born. She usually prefaced the story with her own memory of her long, l-o-n-g period of labor at my birth. Apparently, she never quite forgot the full 24 hours of labor that brought me into the world. And, according to my mother's experience I was a big baby. As she would tell the story, she often emphasized how handsome my father looked, and how well he dressed and the "click-click" of his heels could be heard as he strode down the hospital hallway. She would tell how proud he was as he held me. But the significant part of the tableau was the doctor's line of congratulation to my dad for having a son clearly destined to grow up to be a healthy line-backer for the Buffalo Bills.[1] This seemed to reflect both my birth-weight, of which my mother was so very aware, and the general male stereotypes of the era. Although I clearly did not have a memory of that moment when I was only hours old, the memory was passed on for many birthdays over the years.

In the later years of my own childhood memories (ages 6 to pre-teens) there were birthdays where this story was told and the seeds of this birth story could be validated for me but perhaps remembered different from that of my mother.

As an adult looking back on this parent-child dynamic and early childhood development, I grew to understand that there was something rather basic about the nurturing and emotional attunement that was a little out-of-sync from the very beginning; not in any malevolent or psychopathic way, but in the way that you and your dance partner just don't seem to hear the same music. In this parent and child "dance" of emotional attunement, father, and son, we were often a bit out of step.[2] There will be more to the father and son dynamic in the next chapter.

And while we are still within the first few hours of birth, it should be noted that my name was my mother's call with a nod to my father in sharing the same middle name, "John" and that of his father before him. I was named after Doctor Val Deco, an eye surgeon in Buffalo NY. Dr. Deco cared for my mother as patient even in his retirement. My mother was born without sight in one eye and a benign growth in that eye. Dr. Val Deco managed her care from infancy so that there was no facial disfigurement — only a slight discoloration in that eye. My mother named her first-born after him. Even as a little child I can remember making trips to his home in Snyder, an upscale suburb of Buffalo NY. In the 1950's his home with tennis courts and a pool was a glimpse into life of those above my parent's pay grade, but, given the "American Dream" not entirely out of reach. There was, from the beginning some unspoken expectations even in the name that I carried.

In these pre-school years there were signs that indeed I was "my mother's son." Christmas memories and photos from the time show my brother and I dressed in "night-shirts," made by my maternal grandmother, male versions, in stripes and flannel patterns, of a night-gown for boys. I remember my brother and I each had dolls, male dolls mind you, named Jimmy and Johnny. This was at least a decade before the 1960's action-figure toys like GI Joe were popular for boys. Jimmy and Johnny were our little companions and, in retrospect, dressing, and watching out for them, was our introduction into the art of caretaking. Perhaps my parents were leaving an opening for a new developing sense of masculinity. Even in my adult life I have never heard of young boys — children who had "boy-dolls;" action-figures, yes, perhaps, ten years later little boys might have someone to fight imaginary battles or leap tall buildings. But I know of none where such essential life and caretaking skills were developed in little boys.

In our time, my brother and I did have our share of cowboy toys, where we would become the "action figures." But for me, even at this young pre-school age, I was more interested in the cowboy's horse and boots than the rifle or six-shooter. One of my earliest treasures was the gift of a marble horse that I had admired. This, it should be told, was not a toy. It was an *objet d'art* to be placed on the bedroom dresser and admired. And I did admire it for many years, into my college years where it met an unfortunate fate.

In these earliest years, Dad was more of a silent partner. Present and watchful but without much voice. One story, again told by mom, was of a frequent dinner table mishap. It seems my brother and I often spilt our milk on the table at dinner. One-night Dad had had enough! As the story goes, without a word he left mom to clean up the mess while he stormed out of the house — and to the local variety store — where he purchased two "tommy-tippy-cups." These little gifts from heaven were made for parents with young children, so that little tikes could learn all the fine motor skills, grace and coordination needed to drink from a glass but were immune from tipping over. I do remember my tommy tippy cup, and I do remember my father's exasperation. Obviously, he had seen them at some earlier time, he was gone and back within a flash. Clearly, he was an active parent but often silent.

Dad made several attempts to work/play together with my brother and me in these early childhood years. The Erector Set that Santa Claus brought one Christmas was perhaps a toy a bit advanced for my abilities at the time but more importantly it did not fit my interests. I do remember Dad made a great motorized Ferris wheel while I handed him the pieces he asked for. And I filled the seats of the Ferris Wheel with characters from our other toys when it was fully operational. Dad attempted to teach us how to build a bird house — I watched — and I may have painted it, once it was assembled. But even at an early age my interest in things mechanical was lacking. Still to this day I am hopeless with hand-tools.

While examples of a disconnection of father to son were plentiful, the pattern that developed was one of a benign paternal distance; well-intended but unsuccessful attempts to connect through the usual father-son tasks. In later childhood, I was aware of disappointing him in most sports. This was evident, not so much because of any displeasure shown on his part but rather because I was so aware that dad would present me with things that I had not asked for nor shown an interest in, and I would proceed to abandon any interest in them. The erector set was a good example, and later, a baseball glove. As I grew to appreciate myself and my skillset as an adult, I was more aware of the pain of not-knowing what to do, that he must have felt in those early parenting years.

Dad's approach had perhaps an unintentional consequence; I grew-up finding alternative father-figures in my camp counsellors, teachers, parish priests along the way. At this early age I was not aware of my search based on something lacking in my father. I was more aware that something just "clicked" in these role models for me; there was an attraction like that indescribable sense of being drawn upward by the line of gothic architecture, eyes rising to the sky. From an early age, I became at home with an extended "family" of professional caregivers. In fact, stumbling into several alternative guides or father-figures along the way, where they would respond to me based on my interests or my questions. These became the norm for me. Perhaps dad was a quick study and discovered that his role was to place me in a proper setting and let professionals take over. This became his approach in later childhood and teen years for hunting rifles, sex education and driver's ed.

My innate interests tended more toward art and music; beauty attracted me rather than the thrill of speed or strength. And while early undiagnosed vision limitations did make sight-reading music difficult, I preferred to plod through a musical staff cautiously note by note, and I found that after one or two passes on the score, I could play it from memory rather quickly — perhaps to the detriment of developing good sight reading skills but more on the piano later.

There were two areas where dad and I did connect in these pre-school years. Two areas where the senses made the connections for us, overcoming whatever cognitive dissonance there was at this early stage. Touch and smell are my earliest memories of my father.

There is a photograph, now lost, but vivid in my memories. In pre-school years, there was a designated time just after my father returned home from work. As I remember it, Dad must have freshened-up when he got home from work because he always smelled good. I remember Old Spice, which would have been popular at the time. And in my teens, Brut Fabergé, was dad's gift to his pre-teen-aged son. It has been interesting to me, that while memories of early bonding through tasks were scarce, there was a scent that was unmistakably "Dad."

In my second book, *Le Petit Jardin de L'âme*, I tell of a time where I returned to my parents' home shortly after my dad's death in April of 2008. I slept in the spare room and used the second bathroom, which, as it turned out, was the bathroom my father had used on most days. It was so recent after his death that there were still some of his toiletries in the medicine cabinet. During the first morning after my arrival as I shaved and showered, I noticed a small bottle of Brut cologne. There was a magical moment, a form of "anointing," as I, without hesitation, now the elder Littman, applied a touch of Dad's eau de cologne during my morning ablutions. If my mother noticed anything at the breakfast table, she said nothing, but I was aware that I was "wearing" essence of Dad.

Another indelible family ritual from these pre-school years is vivid: While mom made last minute preparations for dinner, Dad, my brother, and I would have a "free-for-all" on the living room floor. As I remember, many of these ad hoc tussles began as a "tickling match" but they always ended with a raucous wrestling match. This "rough-housing" was to some extent staged and dad made sure there was some loose change to fall from his pockets. It was one of the few times I can remember being totally at ease and having fun together as we tickled and wiggled on the floor or on the sofa. The goal was for my brother and I to tip him upside down and then dash for the cash. However it began, it always ended with warm hugs and smiles — and a little extra cash for the piggy bank! It is my fondest memory of my father and one that I called to mind in young adult life — usually when I needed some antidote for confusion and emotional estrangement that developed between us. In retrospect, this bond was something unconventional for the 1950's male. While the expected male contact through sports did not appeal to me, there lingers a different memory. I have always felt comfortable with a man-to-man hug of affection. And I have always tended to the finer aspects of gentleman's grooming. My dad was a factory worker, a Journeyman Pipefitter at General Motors. As I grew up, I had a sense that there were some overtures from GM to raise to supervisory positions, but for some reason he did not take them. A number of friends gradually rose through GM's ranks but dad was not interested in such promotions. I know he was thought well of by his workmates. And while I did not know the details of his contributions to the workplace, I do remember references to bonus checks received for suggestions or improvements he had made in his work area. But he was not interested in advancing to management. Although his work-life was simple, dad was viewed by others as a gentleman; thoughtful, and well-dressed, and a handsome man. At heart, it was these later qualities that he passed on to me rather than any specific sports skill, trade, or tool.

My parents were generous in providing childhood experiences as they attempted to fill our lives with good memories but with many of them there was an unwritten expectation that this was something I ought to do. We ought to ride the Ferris wheel; I so disliked the feeling in my tummy and the swing of the seat. We ought to build a cart for the soap-box derby; I did not like the building of it, and the thought of riding it down Market Street Hill with the only breaks being straw bales at the end of the run, was unnerving. We ought to enjoy Frontier Town, a child's theme park; there were too many people and too much shooting. I sensed early on that I was expected to enjoy these experiences placed before us and so I tried. When in fact I was often perplexed, or not interested. The experience seemed to be fulfilling a parental or social-cultural plan rather than responding to something that I did in fact enjoy. Often the experience did not fit for me and I found myself trying to do the expected to please my parents. But these; the smell of Dad and the "tickle-match-dash-for-cash" are the ones that I cherish.

"Every life is a piece of art, put together with all means available"
— French psychologist, philosopher, Pierre Janet

A second group of memories from these early years, reinforced throughout my life, began on the very first day of school, Kindergarten.

In retrospect, preparation for school fell into my mother's "job-description." I remember the neighborhood rehearsals during the summer before the eventual walk to school in September. Until the age of 10 or 11 we lived in a city environment — a small city, Lockport, New York. As the county seat, Lockport had some of the amenities of city-life in the largely rural area of Western New York. Lockport retained a bit of a small town feel with close-knit relationships; everyone knew everyone and could tell you who was related to whom. It seems that a small group of mothers organized themselves and their children into a step-by-step walking tour that culminated at the school steps. I would walk with my mother from our house to the house of a nearby playmate (maybe a short city-block away). There we would be joined by mom number two, and moms 1 and 2 would proceed with their own child plus one onto the next house and next playmate. We were joined by mom and playmate number 3. This pattern occurred again and the little troop grew one-by-one, until we reached the Kindergarten destination. There were four or five stops along the way. This was actually a dress rehearsal, for in time, one or two of the moms would drop off and we would gradually learn to continue the pattern on our own. As I write this in the year 2020, such a plan might be thought ill-advised and a risk to child safety in the present day. But in its time, it was well thought out and successful. It also set some expectations for us, that once we knew what to do, we were expected to follow the plan, and look out for each other, even without direct supervision.

As much as I remember this well-organized procession to Kindergarten, it is what happened once we reached our destination that I not only remember as a five-year-old, but was a pattern destined to be repeated throughout major moments of transition in my life.

As we approached the steps of the school, our teacher was there to greet us. There were in truth some elements of that fictional archetypal Mayberry in this 1950's era of my childhood. We had all made introductions with Miss Foster, earlier as part of first-day-of-school planning.

And here my memory and my mother's oft-retelling have an amazing congruity; without any hesitation, I waved good-bye and dashed into the classroom eager to see what excitement lay ahead! My mother, in her telling, was a little tearful; my quick departure did not allow for tender good-byes. She was having a motherly moment of separation, while I was on my way to the future!

And Kindergarten was just the beginning: There were other life-thresholds where what might have been lingering good-byes, and looking back, were in fact, typically characterized by my propelling forward into new horizons. Just as at the steps of Kindergarten, I launched into the first day of summer camp, boarding school at Preparatory Seminary, college, grad school, major moves across country and across the world, and my marriage. Every departing hug in adult life was characterized by this dynamic of my mother's gravitational pull and me breaking loose, seeking a new orbit in a galaxy not so far away.

In my later adult life, I yielded some, to what was clearly a desire of mom to hold on; a hug that lasted too long for comfort, a time of near suffocation. It was indeed difficult for her to "let go." And while I am tempted to give her credit that she learned over the years, with some reluctance, I wonder still, did she learn to let go, or did I learn better to spin free of her orbit. This image came to mind even in my mother's last days. At the age of 91, she suffered her third stroke. It was clear that she was not likely to recover. My nephews advised me that her end was near. I made the journey from the Republic of Panama to say good-byes and stayed a week to ten days. Because of the recent stroke, she had limited means for communication; she lost fine motor skills for writing and was unable to speak. After some days with frequent visits alternating with time to close up her apartment, the time came for me to talk about my return to my wife and home in Central America. It was clear to us both that this was a last good-bye. And though her arms could not hug me, this memory held me fast; after our good-byes, her eyes, stretched nearly out the top of her head, as she "hung on to me" as I left the room.

That Kindergarten year provided another set of stellar moments. Let me digress for a moment into the adventures of piano lessons with Beatrice Fraiser before returning to kindergarten. I had begun piano lessons earlier in the same year as Kindergarten.

Mrs. Fraiser was a lady of refinement. Beatrice Fraiser lived in a grand house in a toney part of the city, appropriately called High Street. Just walking up to the front door was a "bigger-than-life" experience for a five-year-old. The house was also filled with music. Often music from a student who had preceded me was still in the air, or Mrs. Fraiser herself would be enjoying a few musical moments in-between students. Her own son could often be heard practicing his French horn when I arrived for lessons. Other musical instruments filled the public rooms at the front of the house. Mrs. Fraiser taught more than piano, she also inspired parents to introduce children to the wonders of the Buffalo Symphony Orchestra, and classical music concerts at local churches.

My dad played drums with a local marching band and on occasion my brother and I would join my parents on trips to hear musician friends playing at a local lounge. But the symphony and classical music was a stretch that Mrs. Fraiser encouraged in her young students and her students' parents. My parents followed. My mother took us to concerts, taught us how to sit quietly and attentively, listened to recordings of light classics with me and my brother, and made the most of Walt Disney's Fantasia with its animated story line to accompany some of the world's classic treasures. I should say that my father followed silently, making the extra money to afford the new piano. Actually, getting the piano was no small deal. Cost aside, we lived in a second-floor apartment. But the piano appeared as if by magic so that their five-year-old would have the proper tools for learning. And of course, mom and dad, and grandparents in the apartment below, endured hours of repetitive practice for scales, etudes, and "five-finger exercises"- they were saints in this regard.

My enthusiasm for this adventure must have been palpable. Characteristic of this young student and teacher relationship was the name Mrs. Fraiser gave me. She called me Valiant, not Val, but Valiant as in "Prince Valiant" the fictious Arthurian character.

All of this sets the tone for a memorable Kindergarten adventure. One day as a part of the kindergarten activities we were given water-based paints, a large easel, and brushes. We were encouraged to paint anything we liked. In the other children's artwork there was an abundance of stick-people, little houses and trees, and family portraits, as one might expect from budding five-year-old artists. But it seemed quite natural for me to draw a musical staff, treble clef, base clef, and a few notes — whole notes, half notes, quarter notes etc., rests, sharps and flats; an imaginary musical composition; a tableau in the style of a Chagall or Matisse. For me it was a part of my newfound music adventure. But for the kindergarten teacher it was worthy of a trip to the upper grades for show and tell.

The experiences from the early years; of my relationship to my parents, of kindergarten and piano lessons, formed points of light that seemed to forge a path that was to continue throughout my life; knowing that I was loved but indeed different, at times out-of-step, hearing a different drummer from an early age. I felt a double-edged sword; I had the security of being loved but the aloneness of being different. There was always unknow territory that I was eager to explore and the pull of my mother to hold me close. A lifetime of adjusting to what seemed written in the stars was not for me alone, I sensed that the journey was a challenge for my parents also.

It's good to be a seeker, but sooner or later you have to be a finder.
And then it is well to give what you have found, a gift into the world
for whoever will accept it. — Jonathan Livingston Seagull by Richard Bach

The greeting above, was on the card from my parents when, in 1973, I was ordained deacon, the last step on the way to priesthood.

Notes from Earliest Memories:

[1] Football in Buffalo has a long history going back to 1915. But the Buffalo Bills was a newly named team in 1947, the year before I was born. After WWII, when the All-America Football Conference formed, Buffalo was selected for a team; originally known as the *Buffalo Bisons,* the same name as a baseball team and (at the time) a hockey team in the area, the team sought a new identity and named itself the "Buffalo Bills."

[2] Aside from multiple resources on early childhood development; such as René Spitz, John Bowlby, Erik Erikson and Jean Piaget, read for my MSW degree 1978-80, more recent references to Bessel Van Der Kolk, MD, *The Body Keeps The Score* shed light on what he calls this "Dance of Attunement" (page 113 ff) Giving this dynamic a sympathetic metaphor, it was like my parents and I were often listening to different music.

Days of Childhood — Age Six to the "Tweens"

This chapter and this time of my life includes a distinct chronological divide as well as the developmental shift from being my mother's son to being my father's son. While I was fortunate to have both parents present throughout all of my life, well into my 60's, there is a distinctive shift in emotional attachment during these years of primary school and the "tween" years.

The normal developmental attachments were accompanied by a geographical shift. From a time just after my birth until about age ten or eleven, my family lived in a two-flat in the city of Lockport, at 351 Walnut Street. My parents, my brother and I lived upstairs and my father's parents, my grandparents, lived downstairs. I am certain that the house was owned by my grandparents and served as a low-cost, starter apartment for my parents and their young family.

Shortly after my tenth birthday we, my parents, brother, and I, moved into a new-built home in the country, on ten acres of land. There were two ten acres plots specifically purchased to build two homes. My parents' home was completed first and a few years later my grandparents moved into their newly built home next door. This new-built home in the country was the home from which I left, at the age of fourteen, when I set out to the Buffalo Preparatory Seminary; my choice for high-school education, a boarding school and preparation for priesthood. (more on this adventure later)

And so, for these pre-school and early school years my home is the two-flat, upper apartment in the city. And then later moves to the adventures of country-life when I was about 11 years old.

During these childhood years my mother was largely a stay-at-home Mom. Although there are a few stories about her work-life in the kitchens of one of the nicer restaurants and catering business in the city, I do not remember her working outside the home in my early childhood years. Somewhere around my seventh or eighth year and before we moved to the country, Mom returned to school and graduated as a Licensed Practical Nurse.

I remember evenings where my dad was at work, at a second job. And moments of snuggling up with Mom while she studied her nursing books before we went off to bed. I remember the grand event when she had the eye surgery that would remove one eye she had from birth, which was slightly discolored. The nonfunctioning eye was removed and replaced with a cosmetic prosthetic eye, which was so perfectly done as to challenge anyone to discern which was her "good" eye and which was the prosthetic. I remember going to the hospital in anticipation of a great and good event, not a traumatic moment. Doctors and nurses were miracle workers, and the physical care they offered was much to be admired. Hospitals were places of wonder.

As my stay-at-home mother became a nurse, we became a two-income family. This, in the 1950's was still not the norm of family-life in America. I think that, as a family, we were a little bit ahead of the social curve in this regard. It also made for a new division of child-care labor between my parents. I remember, dad stepped up to the task, and he had some built-in reinforcements with his parents living just one floor below. But clearly it was his task, and Nana and Pa (childhood names for my grandparents) were an assist, not our new caretakers.

My grandparents were another aspect of a kind of dual citizenship, growing up in both "Town and Country." While my father's parents lived just one floor below us in the city house, my mother's parents lived on a farm in the country about 20 minutes away.

Even as a child I had a sense that both sets of grandparents took their turns providing some respite care for my parents, the young married couple. Weekend overnight trips to the country farm of my grandparents were always an exciting time, with lots to explore and often other cousins with whom we would play. Farm-life was a great way to be introduced to facts of life; the birthing of kittens and rabbits, gathering eggs, the planting of seeds and even the shoveling of manure were all learning moments. In the city, our connection to grandparents was more frequent but usually brief passing moments. Going downstairs to have breakfast with Nana, let my parents sleep in on occasion. Nana was a little too indulgent and too roughhewn for my mother's taste. Nana had a list of colorful vocabulary, slang expressions and cuss words, that slipped out unguarded and within the hearing of little ears. At a too young age, Nana would give my brother and I our first taste of coffee, highly diluted with milk and sugar. And Nana would often give us a small stake to play "penny ante poker." And we could keep our winnings! Nana was sometimes the arbiter of brotherly squabbles, especially ones that happened outside her back door. There is a story that circulated in the family for many years of how, during a brotherly power struggle over one tricycle shared between two brothers. My brother went to the back-porch steps and cried because his older brother (me) would not share the tricycle. Nana came to the rescue. Her solution was to walk to the corner store with my brother and buy a new trike. For many a year after that, Larry was chided as Nana's favorite. The story also demonstrates another difference between "Town and Country." I am not sure that my mother's characterization is completely accurate but she viewed her parents as having fewer financial means but a generosity of spirit, spending time and cuddling and providing loving experiences while she saw my father's parents as financially well off. My "town" grandparents expressed their generosity in things that money could buy. Sometimes, in my memory I hear these distinctions with a touch of my mother's acrimony. Yes, there may have been some truth to the fact of the financial disparity but to a child it was all good.

It was during these years, somewhere between age six and eight, that there was a developmental shift from being my mother's son to being my father's son.

My father was a sports man. He was not a tall man, but agile and athletic. Snippets of stories about him told by my mother and sometimes by his adult friends, tell me that he was a good swimmer and diver, he was good in a gymnastic sense of headstands, handstands, and flips. He played the typical sports of baseball, and guard positions in basketball. I don't remember any stories about (American) football. From my earliest years I know that he liked hunting pheasant and deer. It was normal that he would try to find a connection with his son and pass on the skills from these areas of his life. But the connection, for the most part, with me, was lost.

I remember dad tried to encourage the typical, and, assumed, affection for sports as a father to son. I do not remember my dad being emotionally demonstrative very often but I do remember his attempts to pass on what he knew as necessary life-skills. A gift of Converse high-top sneakers, a brand-new leather baseball glove (for a left-hander nonetheless), were among the various sport paraphernalia that he used to express his love and certain expectations. Later there was a hunting rifle. I proved woefully inadequate and more importantly uninterested in all of these. Preparing me for the basketball court and for the baseball diamond were for him part of his fatherly pride. Not only did I not like these team sports, but I was also not good at them. Or was it that I did not like them because I was not good at them? Through progressive trial and error and routine parental inquiries, it was determined that I needed eyeglasses. Perhaps this would help to explain why I was not good at playing catch or hitting the ball. But, aside from the basic requirement to actually *see* the ball, I simply was not interested in these team sports. Later, at age nine or ten, it was determined that eyeglasses were indeed needed. But by then there was plenty of "water over the dam" creating memories and little whirlpools of psychological disturbance and inadequacies in the flow of this father and son relationship.

Such a mismatch of expectations and abilities and interests in sport validated the original story of my birthday and the mixed message that my dad held a baby line-backer in his arms. What for many a father and son might be bonding over sports turned out for me — and I believe for us — to be a series of disappointments. Little League try-outs were traumatic for me though I tried not to show it. I was on the "B" team that was made up of all the players that remained after the "A" team was chosen, and once in a while I was put in the left outfield position, though I was happy to sit on the bench and hope that the game would soon be over. At least Dad was not tone deaf, little league lasted only one season for me.

This set of memories, beginning from day-one, progressed through the ages of eight to early teens made for an anthology that might be titled *"Father and Son, Two Expectations, One Relationship."* I come away from these memories knowing that dad loved me, he was not overt in his disappointment or harsh, but I knew. I knew that I was not the budding footballer that obstetrician had proclaimed in the neo-natal unit, I was not a rising point guard or even a decent outfielder. I later came to appreciate just how lost he was as to how to connect with his son. To dad's credit he would try again a few years later when I was considered old enough to join him on a pheasant hunt. More on this later.

There was one area of sports where we did connect: swimming at the YMCA. At about my seventh or eighth-year dad was convinced that both my brother and I needed to learn to swim properly. We had many trips to the beach to paddle and play in the water but to be self-sufficient in the water was considered important. Dad signed us both up at the local YMCA as soon as we reached the minimum age. The "Y" was the first of many occasions where dad would place us both, my brother and I, in the care of professionals. We could easily walk to the "Y" from our home so it was an accessible venue that opened up my world in many ways. I took to swim class like a duck to water and while I was not a budding "Michael Phelps" or "Greg Louganis, "I did well and enjoyed childhood swimming and diving competitions. Over a few years I eventually qualified as a Junior Lifeguard, sometime before we left the city for our new home in the country. And in my late teens, for a summer job, I also qualified as a Red Cross-certified lifeguard.

At the YMCA, my eyes were opened in other ways as well. It was the norm at the YMCA for all swim classes to be conducted in the nude. Swim instructors wore swim trunks and if there were spectators at competitive events, we wore swim trunks, but for classes and free swim times, naked was the norm. I think that at the YMCA I first became comfortable with being naked. Up until now, naked was simply a brief period of transition from one suit of clothes to another. Here at the "Y" I realized that clothes were not necessary for every activity.

At home, my brother and I sometimes bathed together in the large cast-iron, claw-foot, tub when we were small. But I never remember seeing my father naked. Home culture around dress was modest without being uptight. From an early age attitudes toward our bodies was filled with a respect and amazement; even the biological journey from everyday scrapes and bruises through the healing process was chronicled as a marvelous moment. Bandages were not just applied and taken off but the little wounds were inspected and became a biology lesson. As my mother progressed in nursing school, we also learned how to wrap bandages on tricky body-parts like elbows and feet. My brother and I made slings alongside my mother and learned various ways to take a temperature; yes, orally, rectal, axillary, and tympanic. All was a part of a "show and tell," appreciating our bodies. I believe that there was a conscious effort, mother leading the way, but followed by dad in a kind of silent approval, to counter some 1950's cultural aspects of puritanical propriety or inhibition.

From an early age my brother and I learned the proper anatomical names for our body parts and bodily functions; a penis was a penis, not a "peepee," not a "dick" or a "ding-dong," a Bowel Movement was a BM. We knew what BM stood for, and knew it was a medical abbreviation. And so, we were proper in the sense of correct but not prudish. I would be well into my teens before I learned slang equivalents from my peers.

When I was about eight, I received a small Eastman Kodak Brownie camera. It was a first communion present, I think. I remember taking a picture of my brother in the bathtub. As it happened the picture was taken after the water had drained, so, there he was, in all his innocence. It was only when the film was developed, and my parents saw the picture, I learned that perhaps this was not the best idea. My parents, to their credit, managed to express concern and not anger, emphasizing personal privacy not a moral judgement. Perhaps my first remembered lesson in discretion.

But back at the YMCA; I remained uninterested in the usual team sports of basketball and baseball, but while advancing in swim class, I eventually held my own as a member of a swim team. During this time there was some collateral learning. I learned about boys' locker rooms and common shower rooms. Happily, I can report I never felt abused or taken advantage of. Fortunately, all the adult supervision from my experience, was proper. It was at the YMCA that I learned that combination of discretion and a kind of privacy that happens in a room where everyone is naked. How one at the age of seven or eight can learn to take off all their clothes, put them in a locker, walk into the shower room with a dozen others, take a swim class and make the return trip; all with the joy that was intended, no embarrassment, no impropriety. I also learned at this time that I was made just like everybody else, strengthening my self-confidence and body image. Of course, we had towel-fights and other good-natured locker-room shenanigans but nothing we would be embarrassed about in news headlines like those we see today about child abuse or endangerment.

Interestingly, it was about this same time when I did learn that something bad could happen.

A male cousin came to visit us one day. I don't know if it was a planned visit but I do know that it was out of the ordinary. While we knew him well and had visited his family often, it was unusual for him to come to visit alone. My grandmother was watching over us at the time during the "hand-off" time; my mother was out and my father had not yet come home. My cousin was in his mid-teens, eight or nine years older than my brother and me. We were playing in my grandfather's work shed, at the rear of the city lot, so it was not far from the house. It was there that he exposed himself and encouraged us to touch his erection. My memory was one of curiosity, not fear. I was amazed at the size! Upon adult reflection, his size was probably within the normal range but this size was magnified by the fact that I was little and had never seen an erect penis before.

My first clue that there may be something wrong with this picture was that my cousin told us this should be kept a secret. But it was not secret for long. Two things happened. Nana told mom of the unusual visit in the course of relating the day's events and mom was savvy enough to ask my brother and I what happened during our cousin's visit. In our innocence somehow the story of the afternoon just came out. Using a combination of correct medical nomenclature for the body parts I knew, and a child's sense of wonder, I described the events in the work-shed. A brief physical examination by my concerned parents followed. I did not feel traumatized, but I could tell that something was amiss. A visit to my cousin's home and his parents was arranged promptly. During the visit, my brother and I played with my other cousin as usual, while a conversation in hushed tones was carried out among the adults. This was my awakening that both wonders, and mysterious dangers could exist side-by side.

It was about this same time that, in the Roman Catholic tradition of the day, I was preparing for my first communion. At around the age of seven or eight — second grade — this was the norm. My brother and I attended a Roman Catholic parochial school taught by a religious order, the Sisters of Saint Mary Namur. The catholic school was one of many in the Lockport area which tended to be loosely congregated into ethnic groups. This was not an enforced segregation but it just seemed that most of the Germans attended St Mary's, the Irish went to St. Patrick's, the Italians to St. Antony's, and St. John's seemed to be for everyone else Roman Catholic. And of course, the public-school system was available to everyone. The Belgian order of nuns served all the Catholic schools in the area.

It may help to understand all of the schools were predominately white. While, as a child I was not aware of any overt racial segregation, the parochial school system did not include many people of color. I remember no children of color in my class during eight years of parochial school and none in the school yard during recreation times. This curiosity will be explored later in the book because, while it is significant, at this age I was blissfully unaware of an important aspect of my "very white" environment.

An interesting curiosity which remained out of my sight until my late teens, were immigrant laborers. These seasonal workers in the vegetable and fruit farms of the area magically appeared and disappeared each summer and fall. While the ethnic groups that sent their children to the local Roman Catholic schools all wore their heritage on their sleeves, celebrating various ethnic saints and traditions, perhaps only one or two steps away from being immigrants themselves, the local farm labor, harvesting crops were largely invisible.

It was in this environment that I was to begin the moral quest to learn right from wrong. The concept of "good" and "evil" is certainly more complicated than a child can fathom, but it is a life skill that must begin sometime, somewhere. The rather rudimentary aspect of pleasing a parent or displeasing a parent creeps into one's consciousness even in early childhood. And some rudimentary sense of "good" and "bad" does emerge around this age. However, I was now, at the tender age of seven or eight to embark on the first steps of a great journey into moral dilemmas. Little did I know that there was a well laid framework, an entire infrastructure, set by the church to guide even the youngest minds in the beginnings of deciphering moral angst, nagging guilt, one's own basic unworthiness, shame ... and the fires of Hell!

Beginning with memorized prayers and ten seemingly simple rules. Following creeds and commandments; written with words crafted by the scholars of centuries ago, skilled in hair-splitting philosophical truths, which I did not understand, I learned to scrutinize my little life searching for violations in need of confession, penance, and perfection. In one family tale from this time; as my parents inquired what I had learned in school that day, I responded that I had learned the *"postle's creep."* Or, more accurately, this is a seven-year-old's title of one of the foundational creeds of the Christian faith from the late 300s CE, The Apostle's Creed. Although fully memorized, my seven-year-old comprehension of this ancient creed was about as accurate as my pronunciation.

The structural backbone of Catholic indoctrination for children was the Baltimore Catechism, first compiled in the late 1800's. While there were several editions through the years, there were none that spoke the language of a small child. Eventually the Baltimore Catechism would be memorized, each stylized instructional question had a specific answer to learn by rote, year after year, chapter by chapter through eight years of elementary/middle school.

Let me say here, that I am appreciative of my Roman Catholic upbringing. But that does not rule out that given the times and even with genuine good intent, some strange things were handed down, often in mysterious ways. I was just one of many little children molded and forged by teachings that have taken a lifetime to undo, reframe, revise and at times, rebel against. For a moment, here are some of the lighter aspects.

At this young age attempts to shape a child's mind, even for good, can take a rather circuitous route. While some commandments, such as *Honor thy father and mother*, and *Thou shalt not steal* can be adapted to fit the life-experiences of little children, other concepts such as adultery are a bit, well should I say, abstract. Perhaps it was sufficient to know that adultery is something that adults do, but that is a bit obscure. And exactly what does, *"thou shalt not covet a neighbor's wife"* mean to a child? The virtue of purity was apparently very important to impress upon seven and eight-year-olds. In a convoluted effort to impart a sense of purity, as in single-mindedness or acting without self-interest, it got mixed up with lust, personal modesty and "custody of the eyes"; all of which were a bit of a mystery to me. I easily got the idea that purity and impurity had something to do with being clean or not clean. But for me, the connection of clean and unclean to my body had more to do with soap and water than a state of mind. "Custody of the eyes" was a euphemistic phrase to tell us not to stare at something that might be immodest. But not really knowing how one could be immodest all I got was "Don't stare!" The hazard of using such delicacies of speech were more successful in passing on confusion rather than education. I can't tell you how often I must have confessed to "impure thoughts" as an eight-year-old in the darkened confessional, not really knowing what this was. But I did know that I had a propensity for asking many questions that seemed to irritate some adults. I often saw the world as a puzzle given to me to be figured out. I had murky, foggy, and confused thoughts which were often inconvenient for adults to answer, so that must be it. However, as an eight-year-old what was really on my mind was; did God smoke a cigar like Father Albert Winter? Because cigar breath wafted through the confessional curtain on the other side from God himself. "Sins" like cussing and swearing to whatever capacity an eight-year-old has, carried the entire weight of "taking the Lord's name in vain," number two on the big ten list. Idolatrous behavior and blasphemy got all lumped into one little child's mind as really, really bad stuff, whatever they were. So, at the age of eight, I thought myself just skirting the edge of the fiery pits of hell.

Somehow, a miracle in its own way, I escaped paralyzing anxiety, and psychotic guilt that many a stand-up-comic tells happened to countless others. But the road to moral integrity had its beginnings here at St Mary's.

It was during these first two years — first and second grades — at Roman Catholic Parochial School I was introduced to some wonderful and slightly unusual aspects of life. My world of authority figures expanded immensely. Up until this time I had only known my music teacher and my kindergarten teacher as authority figures outside my home. The experiences at the YMCA coincided with these years of parochial school. And while the Young Men's Christian Association imparted many of the same values as the Roman Catholic Church, it seemed the "Y" had less of the "fear of God" and a lot more fun involved. The years of ages six, seven, and eight were a grand expansion of my world.

Among the more unusual aspects that were taken completely for granted by my parents and the church, was exposure to a new dress code. While at the "Y" I learned how to be naked, at St Mary's, I learned that the most important people all wore dresses, and peculiar dresses at that. The sisters wore a traditional habit for the time; black, ankle-length, with veils, and starched wimples. The priests of the time wore traditional cassocks as their everyday wear and significantly more fancy frocks when they were saying mass. Soon, as an altar boy, I would be introduced to a modified version of the cassock when assisting the priest at mass. These forms of ecclesiastical dress were not seen as strange but rather fascinating couture. It seemed that the closer you got to the altar in Church the longer and more elaborate your dress became! Ordinary everyday "street clothes" were for ordinary people. Special people wore special clothes. And even at eight years old I already had a budding sense of becoming somebody special.

I know it may be a bit out of place, and given the references in the above paragraphs, perhaps a bit irreverent. But my adult self in the 21st century cannot help but think that RuPaul probably sums up why I could be confused in my childhood with this dress code.

"We're all born naked and the rest is drag."
— RuPaul

But onward to yet another childhood adventure in learning. St. Mary's was very typical 1950's. In retrospect, the movies of *Going My Way* and *The Bells' of St Mary's* could have actually been written about this slice of my life. There were character's at St Mary's right out of the movies.

Albert Winter was pastor of St Mary's throughout all my years of grade school and into the early years of high school. Father Winter was "cast" in the role of benevolent curmudgeon; the scent of his cigar, if not a cloud a smoke announced his arrival long before his actual appearance. A hand-full of young clergy came through the years, often, newly ordained, to inspire the young, provide some good-humored comic relief and soften the bluster of Fr. Winter. And the sisters; Sisters of St. Mary Namur, teaching at St Mary's filled a variety of roles; grandmotherly Sister Anselm taught first grade forever, Sister Maria Goretti was young and pretty, Sister Denis was a little stern and a lot nervous, Sister Mary Patricia had a Boston accent and played all the boys sports, and Sister Mary Aloysia was exacting with a touch of grace.

My life at St Mary's followed what was probably the normal format for indoctrinating a young child into becoming a valued member of society. A quarterly report card at St Mary's included the usual subjects of reading, writing, math, geography, and history, in which I usually excelled. But it was the bottom of the report card — Character Traits — that held equal, if not more importance than intellect. We were graded by the good sisters on Obedience, Cooperation, Orderliness, Attention and my most challenging area, Self-Control.

As these character traits shout out, there was a lot of emphasis on order and control. There were no areas to evaluate such traits as Spontaneity, Enthusiasm, Creativity. Such was the era, where compliance was prized over "rocking the boat." In general, I learned to conform. I did well in most areas, but self-control somehow eluded me. If I were to guess, self-control meant raising your hand "demurely" when the class was asked a question to which you knew the answer, and waiting to be noticed and called upon, rather than excitedly jumping out of your seat with the answer! Self-control meant not drawing attention to yourself. It meant taking your turn at the chalkboard and only filling in the required letters or figures, without an editorial comment or too many questions. Self-Control also meant no extraneous, creative swirls above or below the lines when learning cursive writing style. Self-control meant not stating the obvious when someone had given a lame excuse or outright lied to cover up some minor transgression for which we were all going to be punished. I was not good at "keeping quiet." I was not so much boisterous as enthusiastic, and curious.

And the people all said sit down
Sit down you're rockin' the boat
The people all said sit down
Sit down you're rockin' the boat
— Frank Loesser – *Guys and Dolls* – 1950 (film 1955)

I had eight years of parochial school practice where I learned suppression and repression, under the guise of self-control. In some future areas, of interpersonal diplomacy, it probably would serve me well. However, establishing self-control also had the effect of repressing inherent joy. I learned to become emotionally circumspect. Somewhere during these early years, I learned that to be "good" meant to be "reserved." In my expression of my more passionate interests and feelings — perhaps one would say I learned to be "understated." I learned from an early age to hold back expressions of exuberance, excitement, and childhood abandon. And I learned the art of "custody of the eyes." The spirit of childhood was being harnessed; tamed unto conformity. I have always believed that this was not a malicious thing. It was just the way things were. The colt must be broken.[1]

In my young adult life, this trait of self-control was so well established that, in later years, I sometimes received criticism from college professors and those who would assess my readiness for priesthood, that I seemed somewhat aloof. I could see where they might have a point. I embodied the expectations of the 1950's and would only gradually arrive, at those different expectations of the 1970's. I had a very well-developed internal caution about putting my emotional self "out-there." This would be stretched during my 20's in a most pleasant and exciting way.

But back to my young self at ages seven or eight. In my environment of the time, Altar Boy training was more available to me than the options of Cub Scouts and Boy Scouts, which were seen, perhaps erroneously, as secular options. It fell to my mother since she was the Roman Catholic to help me learn the Latin responses that acolytes recite when assisting the priest at mass. Mass at the time was entirely in Latin and it was important to have some proficiency at rattling off the responses as swiftly as the priest; rhythm and flow were more important than comprehension.

At St. Mary's, the next few years progressed on much the same trajectory as the first couple of years. But two conflicting elements were about to emerge. At first blush, the two irreconcilable desires could not have been clearly understood by a child, little did I know that this childhood dilemma would play itself out in my adult life.

Girls, girls arrived, or rather girls had always been there, but I began to notice girls around fourth grade — age nine or ten. I had not yet embarked on the adventures of puberty but "puppy love" set in. Until this time girls were just co-playmates in the playground. I always got along well with the opposite sex even before I realized they were the opposite sex.

It may have been as early as fourth or fifth grade that my little heart started a "pita-patter" for Tina. Her twin brother was a childhood friend and my mother and their mother arranged for a few overnights and a few playdates outside of school times along with another mutual childhood friend. So, it was inevitable that I got to see a little more of Tina outside of school time also. There was nothing more to this than puppy-love but it was my first experience of expressing my inner personal feelings of attraction. We were a "known item" among our childhood peers on the playground in a nine and ten-year-old's kind of way. This attraction and budding relationship continued through fifth, sixth, seventh and much of eighth grade and made the seventh and eighth grade "Youth Socials" at the gym particularly enjoyable for me. I was reasonably comfortable and somewhat assured at the school dances when many of my male peers were more hesitant, typical of young teen and pre-teen boys.

Ah, but yes, there was another half, a competing interest, that made for a dilemma. In fifth grade our teacher, Sister Maria Goretti assigned a project around the theme of what we wanted to be when we grew-up. This all seemed age-appropriate and fit well with the approach of the system at the time. I knew clearly, well as clearly as a 10-year-old can know, that when I grew-up I wanted to be a priest. I wrote my essay and prepared my scrap book at home with cut-outs and the finished product hung proudly on the class bulletin board.

I should say, that typical of this 1950's time-frame there was an active church recruitment of boys for the priesthood and girls for religious life. It was common for priests and nuns to discuss this as a real option for families to strive for and to foster vocations. There were posters and pamphlets at church events, in schools, and the catholic press. As an example of this campaign's effect on families, I remember that my mother responded to one of the print ads of the time and received two child-sized priest's cassocks — Jesuit style — one for me and one for my brother. We could dress-up as priests, envision ourselves as missionaries to foreign lands much like children could dress up as firemen, or doctors, or adventurers. Such was the promotion that, from many a Roman Catholic's perspective, to have a priest or nun in the family was a real feather-in-their-cap, a star in their crown with promises of heavenly reward. My expression of a desire to be a priest when I grew-up was encouraged, and supported, even if my parents were a bit at a loss as to why… and what this would actually mean for them. Parental pride pulled them through the unknown even if they could not understand my desire. I give special credit to my dad, a non-church-going protestant of unknown denomination. This must have been quite the mystery ride. To his credit, years later, when I was about fourteen, dad took convert lessons at St Mary's and became a card-carrying Roman Catholic.

I should make a disclaimer here, that my initial reasons and desire, at age ten, for priesthood, evolved many times over in the ensuing years of Prep Seminary, and Theology and then again after ordination and even on into retirement. But let's go back to the beginning.

It is hard to explain the desire of a ten-year-old, but in the years that followed, in subsequent reflections and re-evaluations of this initial choice, I became more aware of what had initially attracted me to priesthood through the process of making decisions to remain or leave this career path. In other words, I perhaps do not clearly know what drove the initial decision but as my constant re-evaluation evolved, I was aware of what I was changing from, based on what I was changing to. (Clear as mud?) In time, as some things became more important to me, they either fit or did not fit with the end goal, priesthood. As I made these choices, I learned during the process what had been driving me to this point and what I was choosing if I continued to stay on track to priesthood. Perhaps, gentle reader, an example from a different life choice will help. A man or woman makes their choice to marry their partner for one reason (or one set of reasons) at the onset, but their reasons for staying married evolve over time, and as these reasons evolve, the previous reasons either fade away or grow stronger. And so it was, my desires for priesthood, became clearer to me as I evolved and re-made this decision every few years. In a more mundane way, it is like finding your way through a maze. In order to reach your final destination, you first need to find that "you are here" spot on the map and then move forward.

As best as I can tell, my earliest choice for priesthood was based on wanting to be part of the mystery, or perhaps more accurately the mystique, that surrounded the clergy. Even at the age of ten, I already had a clear picture of myself as a bit special; not in the sense of being better than anyone else, but rather in the sense of being different; seeing things different, making different choices than most. Clergy were clearly special people and admired for the work they did. They were "center stage" at the Mass that people flocked to (yes, in those days, people flocked to church). Priests had a special language that, as an altar boy I could only barely comprehend, but it was surely powerful. And clergy, in the mind of a child, and for that matter in poetic imagery of the church, called God down from heaven. The priest was also the gatekeeper of the way to heaven for the rest of us all. As I remember it, the title of my fifth-grade essay was "Another Christ"; a bit presumptuous my later-self would say, but it just about sums up what I wanted to be when I grew up.

Aside from the fact that neither Father Winter nor the younger priests had a wife, I knew nothing about celibacy. But at ten, celibacy was not much on this boy's mind.

While my initial desire to be a priest expressed itself at age ten, it would not be until age thirteen (eighth grade) that a clear fork in the road would appear in the form of where to apply for high school. So, in the short term I could follow puppy-love and Tina. I also had an ease with her friends. I enjoyed the school dances and co-ed trips to Castle's Dairy Ice Cream and Soda Fountain on Main Street. And I could steal a few moments on the phone with Tina when I should have been doing my homework. Both "girls" and "priesthood" happily co-existed in my young mind.

At this same time there was a moment in the school curriculum to study the Reformation — or from the Catholic perspective The Protestant Reformation. Clearly this part of history, taught at this time in the 1950's/early 60's had a definite Roman Catholic slant to it, which would be unlearned or further developed in later years. But for now, in the mind of a young boy, this complex time in history was a time of great heroic adventures. One of my heroes was Edmund Campion, Jesuit priest and martyr, another was Thomas More. These were thinkers, not swashbucklers.

Somewhere in the general area of 1961, 1962, it was clear that the friends I had known for the past eight years had a major decision head of them, where to go to high school. For most catholic families, the decision was between De Sales (Saint Francis de Sales) the local Roman Catholic High School or Lockport Senior High, the local public high school. One person in my class would choose a military academy, and I would choose the Diocesan Preparatory Seminary. Tina and her brother were among those who chose Lockport Senior High, it was just a stone's-throw from their home. There was some happy precedent for my choice; it was an exception, but not unheard of. So, my parents and I had a chance to explore with clergy and with a local family whose son went off to "Prep Sem" one year ahead of me. I should say that it was thoroughly due to my own inquisitiveness that I even knew about the "Prep Sem," checking with my teachers and the younger priests. This was something that I brought to my parents. They supported my choice, but my choice was not a response to their suggestions, or urgings.

My choice for Prep Sem was a major decision for a 14-year-old. Every Sunday I would leave home to board at the seminary in Buffalo, NY, and return on Friday evening to my family. There will be more on this Prep Sem adventure, but for now there are a few years to fill in from the time when my family moved from Lockport to the country home at 3821 Orangeport Road, in Gasport, NY.

While I lived only three years at home, on the Orangeport Road, before going to the Diocesan Preparatory Seminary, it was the home to which I returned frequently on weekends and summers over many years, with seminary and clergy friends, and one day with the woman who was to be my wife. Indeed, there are many memories about life at 3821 Orangeport Road. The house was built by my father and grandfather on a ten-acre plot of former farmland. There was another ten-acre plot next door eventually filled by my grandparents' home to the North, and a large lot to the South that remained empty for the next twenty-plus years. A few late 1950's "ranch-style" homes dotted the edge of Orangeport road with acres upon acres between them.

Orangeport Road was a long, mostly straight road running North from the Erie Canal. It cut between large swaths of farmland, that was in transition from farming to residential use. Picture the land across from our house as still cultivated for wheat and corn. The land on our side of the road was being sold for new homes to be built. And the land beyond our property line at the rear, marked by a grove of trees, was also actively farmed. It was country-not-yet-turned-into-suburb. There was a lot of space for a boy to grow, to explore, and to get lost in thought.

For now, I will focus on the years from eleven to fourteen at home on Orangeport Road, so as to follow the chronology of the paragraphs above, through eighth grade.

We moved from the city of Lockport to the country during the summer following fifth grade. My brother and I would continue to attend St. Mary's school rather than change to the local rural public school. Both would involve a school bus ride, so from the perspective of transport, it made little difference. Continued attendance at St. Mary's offered continuity and many of my classmates also rode the bus provided by the Catholic Diocese of Buffalo. The bus route included stops to pick up students from the rural areas for all the parochial schools in Lockport including De Sales High School students.

The most notable change in the morning routine was that now we ate a quick breakfast at home and arrived at school minutes before the class bell rang. In earlier years we walked a few city blocks to school — or rather church — in time for the eight o'clock mass. Daily mass was considered a part of the curriculum. A simple "brown-bag" breakfast in the school basement lunchroom followed, before playing in the school yard before class. Now we would arrive in time for a few minutes play in the school yard just before the school day began. It also meant that my serving at the altar as an altar-boy would be limited to Sundays rather than the daily roster. On occasion, we could keep after school activities in town because we could walk to our grandparents' house since they remined in the city for a few more years. However, on most days we made the return bus trip back home to Orangeport Road. We were one of the first to be picked up in the morning route and therefore among the last to be returned.

While the house was built by my father and grandfather, the entire family, extended family, and friends were involved in some way over a few years on this project. The land was flat and treeless. My mother remembered that once upon a time her dad had farmed the land before the great depression. But now, through her eyes, the land had been over-farmed and the soil worked to death. From the digging of the basement and laying the foundations to landscaping, planting a garden, and building the pool, most things were accomplished by "throwing a party" and everyone pitched in. This was not as organized as an Amish barn-raising but, that indeed, was the affect. It also meant that long after the roof had been raised, the wall-to-wall carpet laid and the kitchen cabinets hung, the house on Orangeport Road was a party house, a lively gathering place for my parents and their friends and also for mine in years to come.

One of the earliest memories of the home at Orangeport Road was that we could choose our respective bedrooms and their décor. But within the first year of our move to the new house, my mother's widowed, sickly mother came to live with us. Nana Lewis was congenial and dearly loved, and loving, but her health deteriorated quickly after Pa Lewis's death. She moved into my brother's room and he moved into my room so we were roomies once again. By this age there were brotherly brawls on occasion but we were close. We would put on little shows for our grandmother at times when she would be taken from her sick bed to a comfortable chair in the living room. In winter we would entertain her while she looked out the large picture window. And during one severe winter storm, which took the power out for many hours overnight, we kept a check on her to make sure she stayed warm as we all "camped out" in the living room near the fireplace. After Nana Lewis died, Larry returned to his room but when a favorite Aunt and Uncle came to visit for a few weeks as a part of their annual migration to Florida, it was Larry who got bumped from his room — again. I guess this was the lot and portion for the second son. No one seemed to question that this might be unfair, but in retrospect it was just one of the many eldest son privileges that I enjoyed without really knowing it at the time. I began to appreciate the subtilties of his second-son position, later in life with new perspective. We were both loved and many things were consciously given to us equally. We were only fifteen months apart in age, so we did most things together, but there were differences that come with being "The Eldest." Even if the eldest might not be aware at the time; perhaps the second son was.

Life on Orangeport Road had many a picturesque moment; boy meets world and wonder. One of the parental promises made to us was that we could have pets when we got to the country. And Noah's Ark was opened wide once we got there. A dog, Polar, mostly white, mongrel with springer spaniel characteristics, and a few cats were first. For a few years, my brother and I had a chicken project for which my father and grandfather built the chicken coop. And then there were the ducklings that we won at the local summer fair. The ducks grew up to be Dickie and Della Duck, and so there were a few ducky ducklings that followed. But our prize was Gertie the goat! One year in the spring my brother and I decided that we would "go on strike" until we got a goat. Unionizing for a goat was our compromise position since we had been unsuccessful in negotiating for a donkey. Well, we must have hit a weak spot, since that Easter my dad surprised us with a goat. We named the goat "Gertie" since we had only recently learned that mom's middle name, of which she was not fond, was Gertrude! A memorable scene of life on Orangeport Road included frequent hikes that my brother and I would take with our menagerie in tow; Polar, Gertie, and Dicky and Della explored the undeveloped part of our property, and into the stand of trees at the property line, and on occasion down to the wandering creek some distance away. Polar and Gertie were avid hiking buddies but we sometimes had to carry the ducks.

We also met new friends of the human variety. Down the road, a few acres away, lived another family. Their dad worked with my dad and two sons were about our age; Jimmy was a year older than I and his brother Jerry the same age as my brother. It was with Jimmy and Jerry that we began to explore other areas of the wild. Our new friends were a bit more mischievously creative than my brother or me. We were introduced to new "games" like "who could take off their clothes the fastest and run through the cornfields naked," just because we could. It was with our new friends that I first tried smoking a cigarette — I didn't like it then, and that experience alone helped me to never pick up the habit. I learned a new word when my penis became a "boner!" And we discovered the local swimming hole for skinny-dipping. As boys in their early teens we shared stories and campfires while camping out in a tent in the wild.

Well, actually the tent was set up only a short distance from our house, but it was our world for the powwows of early puberty. Jimmy and Jerry brought out a bit of the inner Huck Finn, nothing really bad, just breaking a few taboos.

One summer, my dad would try again to pass on some useful male-bonding skills by gifting us with 22 caliber rifles. Lessons followed along with target practice and instruction on gun care and cleaning. A few years prior to this gift, my brother and I would join dad in the annual pheasant hunt with his adult friends; not as shooters, but as "bird-dogs" who walked the corn fields ahead of the hunters to scare up the birds and to retrieve the birds if the hunters were successful. My dad made the logical connection that I would like hunting; I did not. What I liked was walking through the fields. I enjoyed the hunt, not the killing.

But another of his ideas was a real winner; Camp Keenan, run by the YMCA. A brief experiment one year earlier with a day-camp for city kids, Camp Pioneer, had been a success. That led to a two week stay at Camp Keenan the following summer; two weeks in supervised cabins with peers, on the shores of Lake Ontario. My brother and I so enjoyed Camp Keenan that we lobbied for four weeks the following year. I had no idea of the costs but eventually realized that this only happened with a bit of financial stretching on my parents' part. It did provide some benefit for them in having a few weeks "off" from parenting. But this, without speaking, spoke to their constant effort to expand our horizons as children.

Camp life was a success in many ways. Most importantly, I could excel in swimming and diving and I did like water-polo, a rare exception for team sports. I remember feeling very proud of myself, and very happy to see the mutual pride that dad felt when I collected several blue ribbons at the Awards Night Campfire for swim competition. Something more happened a Camp Keenan. One year, as my parents came to pick us up at the end of the season, the counselor asked for a few moments to speak with my dad before he got into the car. On the trip home mom asked dad what it was that the counselor had to say. In a kind of private moment of conversation, if one can have a private conversation with four people in the car, dad shared that the counselor noted that I had demonstrated leadership abilities over the course of the camp period. The counselor simply wanted to acknowledge that and encourage my parents to foster it. I had only a faint idea of what leadership abilities were at the time, but I could tell it pleased dad.

This tableau of the 1950's did have some shadows. I was not so aware of this at the time, but my parents must have been a bit stretched and stressed, new home, new expenses. A two-income family meant two full time workers coordinating shift work schedules to cover getting my brother and me off to school, and for someone to be home when we got home after school. To my parents' credit, I grew up feeling like I had everything that a kid could want. In one telling comment from our new playmates down the road, Jimmy once expressed how much he liked coming to our house. To my mother, he said, "I like coming to your house. At your house everything works. At our house everything is broken." But having everything perfect took a toll.

We went through a couple rough patches in the new house. There are two particularly memorable, and decidedly not *Leave-it-to-Beaver* or *Father-knows-Best* moments.[2]

At my mother's new job at Mount View Hospital she became friends with a doctor from the Philippines. Dr. Santos (I will call him). We received gifts from Dr. Santos, sometimes just little treats, but a new hi-fi stereo system, an upscale option from a phonograph turntable, was a gift, apparently given to us because it would not fit in Dr. Santos' apartment. My mother loved to fill the house with music. Dr. Santos also offered to take my brother and me for a weekend at his apartment giving my parents a "weekend off from parenting." This was still a time when some doctors were provided a residence on site. Since this was a former TB hospital and sanatorium the grounds were extensive. Staying with Dr Santos was an adventure, complete with a mini hospital tour. But most memorable to me was that while staying at Dr Santos' that weekend I learned to tie a tie, a Windsor knot, and proudly showed off my new skill when I got home. Since I did not yet have a full-length tie of my own, (mine were still of the "clip-on" variety) I had one of Dr. Santos' ties that he gave me. My dad became suspicious, it was not immediately clear, suspicious of what, exactly. But the sounds of the midnight argument a few days later that could be heard from my bedroom; made it clear. Amidst the shouting and the angry whispers and the threats of suicide, all the stress came rushing out. Yes, Dad accused Mom of an affair. I don't think there was one. Yes, Mom threatened to leave; she did for a couple days. But the most threatening thing was that I learned my dad had a gun! Not a hunting rifle, a HANDGUN in his drawer! No, he never used it and, in my memory, got rid of it shortly after the argument. The next morning everyone played a game of denial. Mom was gone; briefly visiting some friends, Dad said, something had come up. She would be back in a few days; he said with as much confidence as he could muster. As far as I can remember no one ever mentioned this horrible night, although I know from brief comments in my adult life that it had a big impact on both my brother and me.

Upon reflection, this midnight argument was one of only two parental arguments that stand-out over my parent's sixty years of marriage. The first happened when I was much younger (pre-school age) and when we lived in the city.

The first parental argument of note came, when we lived above my grandparents. While my parents fought, my brother and I crawled from my bed and snuck down the back steps with little shivers of fright and crawled into my grandparents' bed. I am certain that, in the morning my grandmother had a "sit-down, head-to-head" talk with my parents, and it never happened again — until it did — years later.

In retrospect, beyond the moments of fear they inspired, both incidences had the impact of dissolving a child's image of parents as god-like, perfect, and all-powerful. While the parental arguments were few and far between, their impact was big; the arguments chipped away at confidence that my parents could do anything, and that they would make everything alright. Also, the arguments made an early emotional connection to expressions of anger as "bad," destructive, forbidden. For the longest time, it seemed that the best alternative to anger was "containment" and indefinite suppression, until one simply exploded. In my adult life, I searched for satisfactory expressions of anger — sometimes I got it, and sometimes not so much.

My parents were more of "where there is a will there is a way" kind of folks. They were problem solvers. So, it is strange how, in the midst of other positive examples of problem solving handed on to me by parental example, these two exceptions carried a disproportionate weight and impact.

But back to the house on Orangeport Road and approximately age twelve. A different decisive moment of anger rose up. It was a father-son moment. My parents generally used a persuasive style of discipline; when reason failed to produce the desired change of behavior, giving, or taking away privileges was "Plan B," but a spanking was not out of the question when all else failed. And yes, my father was usually the enforcer. I was slow in reconciling one definitive father-son moment, and it looks like, even in this book, I will delay it just a little bit longer.

Let me take a little lighter diversion here, before getting to this father-son moment. The following tale gives you some sense of my innate personality, that apparently needed taming, trimming, and pruning.

My mother told this story with humor about pre-school days. She was attending Sunday Mass with both my brother and me in tow. We already knew that church was a place of quiet but that did not stop our occasional giggles and wiggles or squabbles as young children. In an attempt to separate me from my brother and regain the required solemnity, my mother picked me up in her arms and, in an Irish whisper, informed me that if I continued to act badly, I would be pinched. I decided to test the limits, and mom, in turn, gave me a pinch. But I was not to be outdone. I announced to the entire church in my "outside-voice" with a cry "Mommy, stop pinching me." She was mortified, and a slight adult giggle rustled through the surrounding church pews. A meek and mild little child I was not.

Now I return to a more serious encounter that lay ahead. Around the age of twelve, some grand disciplinary moment arose. I do not remember what the infraction was, but I do remember that I clearly maintained I was right and began to resist the usual parental persuasion. "Talking back" was not allowed. My father, in exasperation, grabbed me by the arm and tried to bend me over to receive a spanking. I resisted further and in addition expressed my rebellious indignation. Now, whatever the original infraction, I had just "upped the ante"; the tensions escalated. My father pursued, I resisted, and my mother on the sidelines was crying "Stop, stop." The fracas that ensued; grappling and pushing and kicking, were brief but it became clear that I was now too big to spank. Yes, I was sent to my room. I went in a huff, but a part of me felt that I had prevailed. It was clear I was no longer a little boy; I was indeed a handful for my dad. In a protracted fight I would not yet have the muscle to endure, but in this scuffle, I had just asserted a different and significant strength.

The heat of the moment drifted away, but the father-son differentiation was definitive. I felt I had made my point, and my father was rendered a little less omnipotent. I was growing up.

Every boy, in his journey to become a man, takes an arrow in the center of his heart, in the place of his strength. Because the wound is rarely discussed and even more rarely healed, every man carries a wound. And the wound is nearly always given by his father.
— John Eldredge, *Wild at Heart*

Growing up in my family, there were seldom moments of direct apologies. The unspoken rule was a period of silence and distance, followed by little gestures that brought us back together. And that was how the next fifty years of father-son relationship would be lived out. Inch by inch, a little act of kindness, followed by another little act of kindness, we recovered some healing, albeit never fully acknowledging in words of apology, the power of the moment in that last spanking.

These two events of anger and argument around age twelve were critical in defining who I was coming into being, but they also set on course a new definition of who my parents were to me. I was growing past their realm of influence. My decision to attend Prep Sem, further defined that growing apart. With my choice for Prep Sem, I was entering a world very different from theirs. The geographical distance was little more than an hour's drive, but I was embarking on a life-journey to lands unknown. Yes, unknown to me but with much unknown also to them. We were, in fact, fellow pilgrims into this unknown. But I believe that they, from that time forward, felt that we were really to live in two very different worlds. It was through entrance to Prep Sem that I became more aware that my family of origin started to become a smaller and smaller part of influence on my life.

Notes from Days of childhood – age six to the "tweens"

[1] "Breaking" is a shortened form of "halter-breaking." It refers to the process of taking a young horse and training it to accept first a halter or bridle, then saddle and rider — basically, turning an untrained horse into one which is trained and suited to a particular purpose. The word *colt*, is being used here as in young male horse, not the firearm. These terms were familiar to me from time spent with my uncle and cousins on my mother's side who competed in western-style, horseback-riding competitions.

[2] These two 1950's TV shows were contemporaneous with my growing up. And many aspects of my real life looked like the family on the TV screen; including the ability to hide anything unpleasant.

Diocesan Preparatory Seminary Days

The preparations for attending Prep Sem began much like the preparations for Kindergarten and Primary School; a trip to visit and tour the school, and a few conversations with other families who had sons that had gone a year or two before me. We were all forging new territory.

Before we go further to figuratively describe this new adventure, let me give you a bit of the "lay of the land," the physical territory. There were some students who lived in the City of Buffalo who could commute to Prep Sem much like any high school student would commute. These commuting students were called "Day-Hops." Because I was a boarding student, a "Boarder," I was to arrive the night before the first day of school in order to get settled into my place in the dormitory. My parents came into the dormitory as did other parents that first night. It took little time to settle, there was little to settle. The dorm was approximately 30+ beds arranged in two rows, each with its own metal dresser, a metal chair, and a locker against the wall. Perhaps this style of décor would best be described as "Military Chic" or "Monastic Minimalist." So, here we were. That's it! Thirty-plus, fourteen-year old boys in one big room. Oh, yes, the dorm was also occupied by an aged steam radiator heating system that groaned and clanked in the night, sometimes eliciting mimicry or sexually suggestive sounds from those who were supposed to be sleeping.

Two upper classmen, appointed as "prefects" were to guide us, answer questions and handle minor discipline matters. They had the same accommodations as everyone else, except they had priory to commandeer an extra locker. An adult faculty member had a separate small apartment a short distance away on the same floor. There was an adjoining room lined with about 15 sinks, and a toilet-room with about five stalls and approximately the same number of showers. That was the dormitory. Multiply that layout by three floors of the same, and that was the residence hall for the high-schoolyears. On the ground level of the residence hall there were study halls, a couple administrative offices, and access hallways to the chapel building in one direction and the refectory building in the opposite direction.

There was another building, laid out in similar fashion, that housed students for the first two years of college, but more on that later.

My good-byes on the first night at school followed that same pattern as my departures in recent past, with my focus on where I was going and my mother resisting the separation with an overly long hug and a few discrete tears. My father remained rather stoic. Although I would return home the following weekend it seemed like a significant break. Over these high school years, the

Sunday night drop-off and Friday reunion grew more independent. At first my parents would make the journey to drop me off and pick me up at school, but in time, we carpooled with parents and students who were a year or two ahead of me and shared the Sunday and Friday drives. Eventually, on Fridays, I walked from school through the city neighborhood, to a pick-up spot on Main Street to catch the Greyhound bus for trips from Buffalo to Lockport, meeting my parents and brother for dinner in Lockport before arriving home at Orangeport Road.

I dove into seminary life much like I entered Kindergarten, and much like I dove into swimming at the Y. There were many "firsts" at high school seminary. As a "Boarder," life was more regulated than for "Day-Hops." The blend of military school, and monastery had the added interest that we were all teens. Clergy faculty lived in a separate building, with the exception of those who served in the apartments on each floor of the dormitories. But we all, faculty, and students alike, came together for regular prayer in monastic style, morning prayer and mass, vespers, and compline. At the time, these prayers were largely in Latin following the Roman Catholic church calendar.

A typical day went something like this: We were awakened early. I never was already awake, so my morning began with an unceremonious flash of light from overhead, and the Prefect's greeting "Laudetur Jesus Christus" (Praised be Jesus Christ) to which we all groggily responded "In aeternum Amen" (Forever and ever, Amen /so be it). We had about 20-30 minutes to get up, make our beds. wash, brush teeth, perhaps shave, and dress; all while jockeying for a position at a sink since there were about half the number required. Eventually a certain pecking order was established and we were all able to be at morning prayer in the chapel on time. It was important to accomplish this methodically and quickly because there was no time to return to pick up anything left undone. The day began and kept moving forward. Most days morning Mass followed morning prayer after which we went directly to breakfast, following breakfast we had about fifteen minutes free time. This was more like a brief time to run to the toilet or gather belongings from study hall and get off to the classroom building. Classes were very much like other high schools, period after period with a few short breaks for changing rooms and professors. The curriculum was a liberal arts curriculum, heavy on the classics and light on the sciences. There was only one tract since we were all headed for the same goal. Lunch came around mid-day, cafeteria style followed by afternoon classes. Classes ended around 3pm. With 90 minutes of free time. For some, this after-school free-time meant sports, for others it meant glee club, for some it meant some shared study time. All other study halls were periods of silence, each student at a desk in a great room, monitored by a senior student. The 90-minute free time was concluded by assembling for an hour of study hall, followed by chapel for vespers, followed by dinner. A brief period after dinner usually found many gathered in front of the TV for the news, some were interested in the sports section, others in current events. After the evening news, two hours of study hall followed, with a short break in-between. The last study hall was followed by a return to chapel for compline from which time we held the great silence — Silentium Magnum — and returned to the dormitory for night time toilet, and "lights out" accompanied by the prefect's "Benedicamus Domino" (Let us bless the Lord) to which we responded, in chorus, "Deo Gratias" (Thanks be to God). Punctuality was paramount, and self-control tested or strengthened at every turn. As you can see there were long periods of silence, not only during the Grand Silence, but study halls and chapel also required silence.

Such was the basic weekday schedule as a boarder at Prep Sem. As time went by there were a few modifications. Beginning in sophomore year my tenor voice was noted, and I was recruited by an upper classman to chant the morning mass for the convent of nuns who lived on campus and prepared our meals. This was thought to be an honor, but it meant getting up even earlier, and dressing in the dark so as to slip out of the dormitory for their mass which began even earlier than our first call to chapel. There was a rota of choristers in groups of two or three, that would provide the choral parts for the sisters' mass celebrated by a faculty member. It also meant, on occasion, using the 90 minutes of free time after school to learn the Gregorian Chant selections for the choral parts, since mass was still in Latin at that time. This was truly old-fashioned tutoring. One student to another would pass on the ancient chant modes and melodies to the student on the rung below. On occasion the glee club director would assist if necessary, for accuracy. But one clearly had the sense that this was a literal handing down of tradition. In junior and senior years, and college, I was a member of the glee club, and became one of those veteran choristers handing down the traditions. I would also acquire other interests as the editor of the school newspaper and president of the student council, a member of the dramatic reading society, and a member of the fledgling drama club. I was a happy, very busy, student.

Seminary suited me in many ways. While there were the sports-minded "jocks," with a typical gym, and opportunity for team sports that one would expect at an all-boys school, among the many firsts at seminary was an expanded horizon of other interests for young men. Glee club, music, and song in general, was probably near the top of the list. The seminary glee club was the source of the seminary's main fund raiser; responsible for filling 2,800 seats of Kleinman's Music Hall each year and soliciting sponsors. Aside from the musical preparations, the organization of the annual campaign itself was significant exercise in student leadership and camaraderie.[1] Oratory and writing skills were also cultivated, through the dramatic reading society, debate club, drama club, and the school newspaper. Some clubs, like dramatic reading and debate competed with other schools in the state. There was also a sense of political leadership developed through student council. All of these were a better fit for me than team sports.

Buffalo, with its population at the time, a bit over one million, was small enough to get to know, and large enough to have a growing inner city. Buffalo's growth in the past was marked by ethnic neighborhoods. At the time I attended Prep Sem in the early 1960's, the ethnic neighborhoods of the past were moving into the suburbs. The Prep Sem was located on 564 Dodge Street, smack dab in the middle of a growing impoverished inner city. My new life at the Prep Sem, would be my first awareness of segregation, and it would also make me more aware that I had been living in a type of segregated society all along but did not know it.

When we lived in Lockport, the Niagara county seat, I was vaguely aware of a "Lower Town" area of the city, not because I knew anyone from Lower Town but because it was an area that we passed through, on our way out of Lockport to visit my mother's family in the country. My Nana Littman, would sometimes make a reference to lower town with a bit of disparagement in her voice' it was considered not safe, or there might be a reference to something once genteel, a touch of faded glory, but now run-down, in Lower Town.[2] No one in my family ever identified Lower Town with African Americans, and as a child I remember no derogatory slang. But in fact, Lower Town was where people of color lived. And while you might come across a person of color here or there in Lockport's commercial district, there were no social events or any reason at all for us to ever go to Lower Town. This was clearly a segregated society but for a child it was a kind of silent segregation. Once I became aware of this, it began to explain the "all white" school and church I attended and the environment in which I had been raised. I did not know that I was living "white privilege" until I lived in the inner city and came to see that I was not a part of the inner city.

At the Diocesan Preparatory Seminary, I was able to see another version of what had long ago transpired in Lower Town. White flight in progress, was leaving the inner city to deteriorate. I want to say that I never had an occasion where I felt unsafe in the area around the Prep Sem and knew of no crimes that affected us. As time went by, I easily travelled through the neighborhood with confidence. But it clearly was all "black" and I was very "white." And once again I realized there were no people of color in my class. As "boarders" we were cautioned in an oblique way to "stay on campus," "not to go out alone," or "at night." Without saying anything disparaging about the neighbors, it said enough. The neighborhood had a few remnants of the old, once German neighborhood; notably the German bakery only one block away. Our schedule did not allow much time for off campus excursions, but an occasional trip to the bakery was a real treat. But more importantly, this was my first experience of learning to be wary of people of color. Whereas a young child, people of color were largely invisible, now people of color were visible, but the message was one of caution. However, current social and political events of the day soon made a very different impression.

As it happened, beyond the academic courses there was much to learn. The years that I attended Prep Sem were the height of the Civil Rights movement in the USA.[3] The "Freedom Riders" of 1961 happened mostly out of my view. But the events of 1963 at the University of Alabama and the March on Washington and "I Have A Dream" and the bombings at the Baptist Church in Birmingham; the events of 1965 with the assassination of Malcolm X, Bloody Sunday, the Selma to Montgomery March, and the 1968 assassination of Martin Luther King Jr. were in clear view, they helped shape my decision to remain on the path to priesthood. There was a time to question, to wonder where I might be most useful. At the ages of 14 to 17, I was old enough to be aware but not old enough to have any real power. But social injustices, systemic racism and institutional hypocrisy came rushing out of the closet to make their imprint.

I also remember that at the time of the 1963 assassination of President Kennedy, a speedy school closing for the day, sent us all home immediately. The unspoken concern at the time was for our safety.

Beyond the geography of the inner city, and the unrest of civil rights, we were surrounded by the Vietnam war years (1955 to 1973/75). Some of the guys had older brothers already deployed and for others there was a growing realization that Conscientious Objection was a very real but complicated possibility. These events all made for a rather serious and reflective group of teens.

This was also a time of the Second Vatican Council (1962-65); a time of excitement for some who were looking to modernize the church. And a time of great consternation and fear of change for others. I was in the camp of the former, seeking a change and increased relevance.

Upon reflection in my adult life, if there was ever an opportunity for the words of the old Baltimore Catechism memorized in grade school to mean anything, these events were a clear example of what a Sacrament was; for these events made an indelible mark on my soul,[4] and shaped who I was to become. Seeing these events as "sacraments" was also an early indication that I found an amazing congruence of "The Holy" and the "Secular," not a dichotomy of sacred and profane.

During these four years I became more aware of my privilege, owing little or nothing to the person I was, but simply because I was white. Yet a "what to do" about this was not clear. Should I break out of the status quo? Stay the course? Perhaps a career in law would be more useful than priesthood, perhaps psychology or social work would be more helpful. All of these options were "multiple choice answers" to the question of what I wanted to be when I grew up. This search would continue through adulthood; how to help mend the broken and to merge the sacred and profane.

I mention this, as there was an on-going process, a continuing assessment of my simple choice at age ten, that continued to be evaluated and re-evaluated during these years. I was not the only teen in this dilemma. I was perhaps just one of many, each in their own way, searching for a path. I remember conversations with a few peers surrounding the Vietnam war and the draft. At first this was just theoretical, but as we reached the age of 18 the draft became a real possibility in our lives; so, what to do?

Academics and the curriculum were the obvious thread holding us all on course, but there was a more basic search going on inside. And as teens there was always comic relief and the distraction of high-school high-jinx. There is a book written by Leo J. Reiter who attended Prep Seminary for a while. Leo and another student Joe Demers and I formed a folk group in Prep Sem. The music and the lyrics were our first opening to express ourselves in this social justice context. We sang at Kleinman's Music Hall, in second year, I sang with a different folk group since Leo had decided to leave seminary. Actually, in Leo's book, *I am an Ex-Marine* (see the bibliography) Leo begins to address his own searching, from his perspective. But we all, to some degree at Prep Sem, needed to wrestle with the question, what do I intend to do with my life. But in any event, in a lighter vein, Leo covers, in Chapter Eight, *Hello and Goodbye Padres*, some of the teenage high jinx's at Prep Sem. There was plenty of good-natured clowning around. My approach for these high-school years will be less about the humorous antics, although there were many.

I found the environment at Prep Sem encouraged introspection, so there were serious discussions usually out of sight and in small groups of two or maybe three. Within the teenage antics there were serious moments. I remember senior year being one of those checkpoints where guys would re-evaluate whether to return for freshman-college year. There were also big decisions to be made about the draft for Vietnam. By the time we were seniors we had found a few ways to circumvent the discipline system and sneak a private moment after "lights-out." One classmate and I found ourselves in the middle of the night, sitting on the terrazzo floor of the washroom, weighing his pending decision to register as a Conscientious Objector and stay in the USA, or to emigrate to Canada and evade the draft. Roger left for Canada during the summer after Senior year.

It was always clear that not everyone would return to Prep Sem each year, some would make other choices. I remember that near the first few days of freshman year, the entire freshman class met. As a part of what must have been a general orientation, the priest in charge drew our attention to the fact there were 120 of us in that year's freshman class, 1962. Injecting a sense of reality into the moment, the priest/professor made us aware that over the years ahead, between now and priesthood, there would be attritions and additions through the years. His prediction, presumably based on some history, was that we could expect that 12 of us from that room would actually be ordained — a sobering thought for just beginning. In fact, twelve years later, thirteen of us would be ordained from that class. Oh, yes some would drop out every year and on occasion one or two would enter, but his numbers were right on target. Of this freshman class, about one third would not return for sophomore year. There was freshman classes 1A, 1B, and 1C and for sophomore year there were sophomore classes 2A and 2B and by senior year there was one class of approximately 30 people; some of whom would go on to college years at Prep Sem.

A chapter on these Prep Sem years would not be complete if it did not include our teachers. Beyond the subjects that they taught; teachers had a potential for great impact on personal formation. Each in their own way had some competence in the course for which they were responsible; some few were gifted, some were personable, and none, in my experience were inappropriate or abusive. But neither were any of them a person I would choose as a role model or let into my inner most thoughts. Let me explain, since I do not wish this to be some personal judgement of them, rather, they were just a part of a systemic emptiness.

First it should be noted that our teachers were all male, and all priests with the exception of the science teacher Mr. Over. All of the clergy had travelled the educational route that I was going to travel, that is, none of them had specific training as teachers. They were trained as parish priests or theologians. Their air of authority abundant, but charismatic leadership in the classroom was in short supply. Some had personal quirks, some endearing, mostly exasperating. My favorite teacher was David Doyle, second year math, geometry. He clearly liked what he was doing and made math fun. I don't remember him being around too long. Another teacher who seemed like just a normal guy doing a good job was John Mergenhagen, somewhere between a father-figure and a buddy, but he wasn't around too long either. On the other hand, my personal nightmare was Paul Belzer. Fr Belzer taught first year algebra and advanced algebra (in junior year). Fr. Belzer was as flat as Fr. Doyle was animated. And Paul Belzer was around forever! As it turned out, he followed me through prep-seminary, college-seminary, and major seminary. All of Fr. Belzer's courses were a challenge for me, not because they were difficult, but because HE was difficult. His delivery was a halting, slow, monotone. I did my worst in his classes and his medieval philosophy class in major seminary was the only class I ever failed. But I get ahead of myself.

Other profs had special, sometimes endearing, quirks. Pokey (Daniel Pokornowski) was very short with a bubbly personality, but not very helpful as a professor. When asked a question, Pokey's idea of clarification was to simply repeat what he had already said. He did not seem to understand that I was not deaf; I was trying to understand. Cyril Trevett, (*Mon Père Trevett* — French — sophomore and junior years) clearly enjoyed what he was teaching. Cyril Trevett had a bit of a "swish" in his cassock, his mannerisms were exaggerated and clearly choreographed for maximum effect. He was odd, and an easy mark for student comedians, yet he was comfortable in his own skin. Dan Duggan would fall to the opposite spectrum of Mon Père Trevett as far as mannerism go. Duggan was the jock's jock, with a bit of "locker-room" humor on the side, to keep your attention. But he was a very effective teacher for English literature, that is, if teaching to the test (New York State Regents) is what you are looking for in English literature. Francis Baumgarten, taught Latin in sophomore year. Father Baumgarten was a living caricature of his German heritage; playfully giving us a slap aside the head when we made a translation mistake and blustering up and down the classroom aisles.

And, then there was Paul Whitney. Father Whitney carried two roles. He was school disciplinarian and Latin teacher for freshman and junior years. Fr. Whitney seemed omnipresent, as disciplinarian. He would appear at your most unfortunate times, and he was amused at your dismay.

But a common thread through all the idiosyncrasies was an emotional disconnectedness, an interpersonal emptiness. The dean of the Prep Sem, Monsignor Ralph Miller came closest to making an emotional connection, in a grandfather-like way. But a common characteristic of all the rest was an emotional distance, and with that, a denial of anything remotely connected to developing interpersonal relationships, or a teen's sexuality which was developing right before their eyes. Regarding sex there was, perhaps, one exception – biology with Mr. Over. Even then in biology, human sexuality was a passing moment with a static diagram of the human reproductive system. In the absence of dynamic sex education or personal guidance, it is easy to see why a boy's best options for learning about sex were his peers (sharing mutual ignorance) and soft porn (forbidden but available) Here we were, classrooms filled with hormonally charged teen boys, in a thoroughly male environment and not a single classroom hour or individual counsel was devoted to our burgeoning sexuality. Aside from the occasional confessional whisper of masturbation, not a word could be heard about sex. But it was not only sex ed that was missing, even platonic relationships or things like affection and emotions, were all abandoned, deserted on an arid campus.

It was sometime during the early years at prep seminary that I started to put two and two together, "the birds & the bees" and me. Basic math told me that I had been conceived a few months before my parent's marriage. This was not discussed at home nor did I find it necessary to ask. But an added bit of information raised a question that I knew my parents could not answer.

I began to learn that there were certain impediments to ordination in the Roman Catholic Church. It is a complicated area of Canon Law upon which I will not even attempt to expound here. For the purposes of my story it is sufficient to know that as a teen, I had only a fragment of knowledge that there were some conditions that either prevented a man from being ordained, or in some cases prevented him from exercising the ministry. I first learned this in a roundabout way through the story of Father Isaac Jogues, a Jesuit martyr and missionary of the 1600's. As the story goes, during his captivity by the Iroquois he was tortured and his hands were mutilated so that he could no longer say Mass. (At the time, the sacred host was only able to be touched by the thumb and forefinger — eventually Isaac Jogues got a dispensation from Pope Urban VIII, but I digress). This little bit of knowledge prompted me to inquire about impediments to ordination, but *"a little bit of knowledge can be a dangerous thing."*

By my calculations, my parents were married in January 1948, and I was born in May — not exactly sufficient time for the bun in the oven. Nonetheless, I arrived "early." I was not illegitimate, but I had learned that being a bastard was, according to the 1917 Code of Canon Law, an impediment. This combination, of a little bit of this and a little bit of that, got me thinking; was being conceived before my parents were married an obstacle to ordination? And now, in the age before "to Google" was a verb, how does one get an answer to a sensitive question like this?

I have already mentioned that the Prep Sem faculty did not inspire or attract the kind of sensitivity that would encourage me to confide in them. But this curious, creative, and practical teen saw an opportunity for anonymous inquiry and a potential answer. After all, what's a confessional for if not for secrets, and answers from God's representative himself! So, one day, confessions were encouraged frequently, so this could have been almost any day; after my usual list of failings, I stated my facts and asked my question. This pre-internet, incognito search engine gave me the information I needed — in short, no problem. I'll spare you the longform of the lessons from church history; it suffices to say that barring bastards from ordination was a political and financial decision from the middle ages not really a moral judgement. And "early miracles of birth" after only a few months marriage, such as mine, did not pose the same political or economic problems for the church as an institution. While I was relieved at the time, a few years later this question did, in fact, come up from my mother who had labored under the mistaken notion that her and my dad's moment of passion years ago may have made my dream an impossibility. I was glad I had done my research and I had the answer. She was more relieved than I.

The seminary landscape provided structure and discipline, and a good academic education. But it was bereft of practical teen guidance in the art of living. Even so, I was able to find out what I needed to know and experiment my way through puberty. In spite of the interpersonal barren atmosphere of the Prep Sem, friendships did develop between students. A handful of friends, student peers, that I met in seminary have stayed in touch over 60 years. But the sterility of relationships with people who were to serve as role models, is telling of how the church was not equipped to model appropriate personal affection in relationships.

"One thing you can't hide — is when you're crippled inside."
— John Lennon, *"Crippled Inside,"* 1971 album, *Imagine*

Prep Sem years looked and felt much like a prescient 1960's version of Hogwarts without the special effects of wizardry but with a systemic secret spell being cast without our knowing it.

"Control your emotions, discipline your mind"
— Severus Snape, *Harry Potter, The Order of the Phoenix,* J.K. Rowling

It was during my freshman year at Prep Sem that my dad decided to take convert classes at St, Mary's. The new assistant clergy was personable and approachable. Dad began classes with a buddy and longtime family friend. His decision to convert to Catholicism seemed to come out of the blue, but that was probably more a reflection of how we as a family made personal decisions rather than any impetuousness on his part. It seems that, as a family, we made important decisions internally, processed over time, and then made an announcement when all was decided. As a part of dad's new practice of Catholicism, he joined the Knights of Columbus. While I had mostly associated the Knights of Columbus with their ceremonial robes and the pomp of saber arches at special church functions, the local chapter decided to "reach-out" to the members' teen-aged sons. To their credit they decided to arrange an instructional film and speaker morning at St Mary's for the teen boys regarding sex and sexuality. Actually, rather forward thinking for the time. The film and the speaker were decent, and the speaker tried to elicit questions from teens who became typically silent around the sensitive topic. There was also a brief time for the boys, many of whom knew each other from grade school, to mingle and perhaps process the info in their own way. I give the dads an "A" for effort. What I regretted was that that was not what I expressed. When the morning was finished, my brother and I got in the car, and dad asked how we liked the program, were there any questions we had. There were no questions, but I had to expound, that we already had that in biology class with Mr. Over. I said it with "smart-ass" thoughtlessness of a 14-year-old. My dad took it in stride, but I sure wish I could have taken it back and replaced it with appreciation.

I include this bit of contrition in connection with the high-school Prep Sem years not only because it happened in the same time frame, but because it illustrates a pattern, now seen as written large, and often. Somehow in the journey from innate curiosity and a self-confident early childhood, to my teens, there was a taming of the colt, sure enough. But it was not a channeling or redirection, taking a basic good and reframing it for maximum benefit. No, rather it was a repression of that original gift. There were many years of combined family practice and schooled self-control that needed to be re-learned and repackaged in order to appreciate and re-create what was there at the beginning. To make a reference to Genesis, it seems that the institution missed the message of the first chapter, "in the beginning ... it was good." One of my most appreciated lessons learned on the horizon of my later life was to search past the unpleasantness of a situation and look for the good that was being frustrated, repressed, or ignored. Sometimes this applied to me, myself. Sometimes this applied to the unpleasantness of others, or other's actions toward me. I learned to ask myself; What is the good that has somehow gotten twisted, suppressed, or lost along life's way that now slithers out in a most unpleasant way? And sometimes when it is viewed in this way, it is possible to find an alternative to having something to say, to be generous, and perhaps to say little or nothing at all.

"See everything, overlook a great deal, correct a little."
—John XXIII

Notes from Diocesan Preparatory Seminary Days

[1] **A note of clarification**. I was not the leader of this student-led annual fundraising campaign. I was a participant. For other references in this section I was editor of the school newspaper, *The Prep Post*, and president of the student council, and member of the Dramatic Reading Society competing at state level competitions.

[2]**Lowertown Historic District** is located at Lockport in Niagara County, New York. The district is now predominantly residential in nature, with some commercial structures and warehouses. The most elegant homes are along Market Street, east of Chapel Street, facing the Erie Canal. Notable structures in this district include the Western Block Company Warehouse, a 2½-story stone structure built before 1855; Lockport Bank Building built in 1829, and located at 315-319 Market Street; Washington Hunt House, built in 1831 and home to New York Governor Washington Hunt and located at 363 Market Street; the former Christ Episcopal Church at 425 Market Street; and the Vine Street School, an Italianate-style one-room school built in 1864. It was listed on the National Register of Historic Places in 1973.

[3] High school years at the Diocesan Preparatory Seminary were from 1962 to 1966. But an extra note about the structure of seminary education at that time may be helpful. At the time, in keeping with the overall religious vocation recruitment of the day, young men (boys of high-school age) could enter a preparatory seminary, as freshmen in high school. This was much like military schools of the period, preparing young men for a military career. The Roman Catholic system was set up on two campuses, in two, six-year segments. The first segment included four years of high school with a high school diploma and a New York State Regency diploma, followed by two years of college with an associate degree. The major seminary, at the time named St. John Vianney, in East Aurora NY, followed with a second, six-year plan, which included completion of two additional years of college — called philosophy years - awarding a Bachelor of Arts degree. Philosophy years were followed by four years of theology, a post graduate degree of Master of Divinity, a year of internship as a deacon, culminating with ordination to priesthood. Throughout this process young men would enter or leave the process. This is the path I followed from 1962 (age 14) to ordination as a deacon in 1973 and priesthood in 1974.

[4] The Baltimore Catechism defines a sacrament as "an outward sign instituted by Christ to give grace." In the church's continual struggle to give words of definition to spiritual realities, the term "indelible mark" was used in catholic culture. The sacraments that leave an indelible mark on the soul, can only be received once, and have a permanent effect on a person's character. They are baptism, confirmation, and holy orders. Although the catechism does not make the connection, I could see that there were also certain secular moments that marked a person for the rest of their life.

College Years at Prep Sem – a Brief Interlude

The remaining two years at the Prep Sem were equivalent to freshman and sophomore years of college, following high-school graduation. With the exception being, on this campus, in these two years, freshman and sophomore students were at the top of the student totem pole rather than the bottom as would be the case on ordinary college campuses. During these two years, the personal goal was to make it to major seminary in East Aurora, NY, St. John Vianney Seminary. Freshman year college was also an entry point for a few guys who had attended regular high-schools and now decided to enter preparations for priesthood, either as "Day Hops" or as "Boarders." So there would be a few new faces but a high percentage of the freshman college class, would have been those who remained from senior year of Prep Sem high school.

The residence arrangements were the same as the high-school dorms except that they were in a different building; we had a lot more space because there were fewer students. The disciplinarian was a little less omnipresent and study periods more relaxed. After four years of high school on the same campus, a college level seminarian was seen by many, even faculty, as a veteran, "one of us." Somewhere during this time, I was, on occasion, able to drive to school for the week, rather than being driven. My dad was very good at making sure my brother and I got our driving licenses as soon as possible and a car on our 18th birthday. As students who had already known the Prep Sem campus for four years previous, fifth- and sixth-year students also knew how to "work the system" a bit, so there were some off-campus activities that were probably forbidden if they were discovered. Two incidences come to mind that spoke to stretching the rules and stretching our wings as college-age students.

As Buffalo saw gradual decline of its main street during these late 60's, one of Buffalo's Landmark's announced its imminent closing. The Palace Burlesque Theater (or as the Marquee spelled it- Burlesk) announced its closing performances. This was an old-style burlesque theatre from the early 1920's with its showgirls, strippers and comedians à la George Burns and Gracie Allen, Abbot and Costello, and other classic comics. A small group of guys convinced ourselves that it would be seriously delinquent of us to let this historical landmark close without actually knowing what a burlesque theatre had to offer. And so, we embarked on our risqué adventure. It was as one might expect, a lot of hype, a little suggestive and the showgirls were a little "over the hill." Although I was able to tell my parents where I had been exploring, I don't think the professors would have approved. Another night out on the town with a couple of friends was not so funny. One Friday night, in winter, instead of going straight home for the weekend, three of us decided to see what some of the clubs in Buffalo had to offer. We enjoyed mingling with the "in crowd" for a few drinks but at our last club, as we left, we were followed. We knew we were in trouble as we heard voices behind us following us to my car — a classic Triumph rag-top convertible. As we got to the car they approached threateningly. We got in, but as I tried to drive away, they were on top of the convertible, my friends supported the weight on the roof while I turned the ignition and put it in gear as fast as possible. But in a flash a knife came ripping through the canvas. Adrenaline took over. Instantly, the three of us, as if rehearsed, let out a *ki hap* roar, worthy of a taekwondo master. We ejected in unison from the car. I guess our aggressors were surprised and simply fled. Thank God since our next move would have been a mystery to us all.

So, that night I decided to stay at Paul's house since his dad was a cop and could advise us in the morning. From Paul's house, I made one of those middle of the night calls that no parent wants to receive, but they were relieved that I was well and all that needed repair was the convertible top.

From this sample of college extracurricular adventures, is sufficient to say that, in these early college years, I began to experiment with returning to my innate curious self and exploring, albeit on the sly, from watchful Prep Sem authorities. Also, during this time, I was able to benefit from a bit of coed socializing because of my younger brother. It was no secret that I was attending seminary and destined to be celibate, so perhaps I was considered a "safe date" but it seemed perfectly normal to do some dancing. I was happy to escort a friend of my brother to her Senior prom at De Sales, and to join the disco crowd during the summers. My brother and I were close enough in age that we often had the same friends and therefore also often had the same friends who were girls. And later, when my brother, after graduation, joined the US Air Force and was not able to accompany his then girlfriend (eventual fiancée, and my future sister-in-law) to her college prom, I was happy to escort her. While there were moments where I had no doubts about continuing to priesthood, there were other times where leading a normal life seemed a good idea. It all seemed to me to be a necessary part of deciding. And it was a great antidote for the sterility of seminary relationships.

During these college Prep Sem years a curious behavior, that started in late high school, got progressively worse. I could not stay awake in class. In fact, to my friends and those who sat closest to me in the classroom, it became a bit of a joke. And they would alternate between helpful periodic nudges to keep me awake or taking bets on how long it would be before I fell asleep. The problem stayed with me throughout the rest of seminary days. Certainly, my classmates knew. My professors knew; some ignored my sleeping, others capitalized on embarrassing moments, and a few took it as a personal affront. In a rather unfunny way, it meant that I had to catch up on the lectures in my own time by extended reading. There were two insights about sleeping in class;

that the lecturers actually added very little to what the texts already said, but more importantly, when listening to the lectures, rather than sleeping, a student is often able to catch the nuance of what the professor thinks is important and thus likely to be on the test.

In any event, I could not stay awake. I tried getting extra sleep, I tried coffee, tried caffeine tablets, I tried sitting in the front of the class. I tried occupying myself with extensive note taking only to wake up with pen in hand and a line trailing off to the bottom of the page from the last word I heard. In one case, I asked my professor if I could stand at the back of the Greek class, hoping that while standing I would not fall asleep. He declined thinking that I was trying to draw attention to myself. Some classes were more sleep-inducing than others but this was a problem for which I received no real help over an eight-year period, two years in college and continuing through six years of major Seminary. There was not even a helpful inquiry, or an expression of concern. To me it again reflects an interpersonal apathy, or a relationship dysfunction that was system wide.

"Constellations shine with light that was emitted eons ago, and I wait for something to come to me, words that a poet might use to illuminate life's mysteries. But there is nothing."
—Nicholas Sparks, *The Wedding*

On the contrary and ironic to me, there was a period of time (about two years) where I had developed a skin rash and sensitivity that made wearing my clerical collar particularly uncomfortable. I tried different styles for comfort but wherever possible I would skip the collar and just wear my clerical shirt with an open collar. While my uncontrollably falling asleep in class over an eight-year period did not merit a helpful inquiry, my not wearing my clerical collar because of the skin rash, prompted at least one faculty member to comment during my student review, that perhaps this was a sign that I did not have a vocation to priesthood. – Sigh — Such was the environment of the time.

After considerable trial and error, over years, I concluded that I was simply bored — very bored. The straight lecture style of presentation was not for me. More embellishment would have helped, I thought. There were a few exceptions where a professor demonstrated a personal investment in the topic; a departure from the text with humorous or practical anecdotes or introducing historical controversies or trivia helped. But most professors chose straight recited lecture style. Attending a lecture class was a bit like attending an opera hoping to hear famous arias of the composition and only getting recitativo.

It is interesting that in my adult life, this uncontrolled sleepiness, has not been a problem. Nor was it a problem when I returned to grad-school post-ordination at Loyola University, Chicago.

Saint John Vianney Seminary Years[1]

The year of 1968 brought with it many changes for me. In September of that year, I entered St John Vianney Seminary, the major seminary, as a first-year philosopher. This was the equivalent of a junior year in college, and the first of six years of study. But before we walk through these years of major seminary, let me bring you up to speed on what transpired during the summer of 1968. A lot happened in the summer of 1968, which made my first year at major seminary very different than what I would have expected only a few months earlier. The summer months held some big surprises.

It had been my pattern from the age of 16 or 17 to get a summer job. My parents did not insist but somehow it just seemed the right thing to do. This was a step up from simply mowing lawns for a few extra bucks. I was interested in working during the summers and saving up for personal expenses during the school year. My parents and my grandparents were always generous, and Nana Littman could always be counted on for a quick infusion of cash if needed, but I was looking for discretionary income. My first two summer jobs were as a lifeguard at a local quarry turned swimming "lake" and recreational campground. But more financially rewarding were my summers as a hospital orderly at Mount View Hospital and later at Newfane Nursing Home. I generally earned enough to save for the rest of the school year with only an occasional cash infusion from Nana which she called "laundry money."

During the summer of 1968, I caught the eye of a young nurse, at the nursing home where we were working. She was just a couple years older than I was. I say that I caught her eye, since I was not looking for a relationship and I was a bit oblivious to her advances at first. But as the summer wore on, I could see her interest. And if I were to have missed what was becoming obvious to everyone else, an older nurse's aide pulled me aside to make one of those "grandmotherly" candid comments; "She's got her eyes on you honey." I was flattered and, frankly, rather tempted; the opportunity for a hot, summer fling was surely possible. But I made it through the summer a virgin! However, I must admit to a little bit of Saint Augustine[2] in me and enjoyed the struggle.

At the other end of the celibate-in-training continuum, that summer I was introduced to William G. Stanton, the new pastor of a local country church, St Bridget's, Newfane. St Bridget's was a sleepy little country church which my mother's parents had attended and which, as a child my brother and I attended with them when we visited. My Aunt Mary was a parishioner and made the initial introductions. Father Stanton, previously a teacher at Bishop Turner High School in Buffalo, was filled with enthusiasm from the Second Vatican Council and was eager to bring the congregation into the new era. I was a seminarian looking for a role model that had so far been lacking in seminary.

It was a match! I began leading the congregation, with my guitar, in the newer folk style music. The parish organist was progressive and we established a good rapport. Father Stanton eventually won over the hearts of even the staunchest recalcitrant, and the parish grew by leaps and bounds. I had a center front-row-seat for the best parish development I was to ever know. Six years later I was ordained from St Bridget's, after many a good-humored talk about church changes, church politics, and some church shenanigans – oh, to be honest, church corruption. During seminary years, Bill Stanton was one of two priests that I could look to as model and mentor.

Life at St Bridget's with Bill Stanton's informal tutelage was a grand part of what kept me focused on priesthood. His approach to the church was not all a bed of roses. His understanding of church history rivaled any suspense thriller or murder mystery, and he openly shared with me some of the more unsavory aspects of the diocesan church as he knew it. At least if I continued to choose the church, it would be an informed choice.

As it happened, July of 1968, was also the promulgation of one of the most controversial and, in my opinion, a most destructive encyclical, *Humanae Vitae* by Pope Paul VI. At a local level it led to many a late-night conversation in St Bridget's rectory among clergy and seminarians and lay persons. Bill was a magnet for drawing in the most interesting and talented of people. It was through my relationship with Bill Stanton that an appreciation for critical inquiry and a form of conscientious objection within the church developed. It was a period of discernable angst in the church; the difficult decision making of people like the Berrigan Brothers, Dorothy Day, Charles E. Curran, Rosemary Radford Ruether, and a growing list of other dissidents, became clearer to me. The dirty laundry of the Roman Catholic Church was beginning to show; often hung out on the lines of every major newspaper. It was at this time that I began to value an integrity of spirit, even if it conflicted with the status quo. This, for me, made the church an exciting place to be. There were going to be interesting times ahead and I now considered myself fortunate to travel along in good company.

As it turned out, the Encyclical[3] (see the note below) opened major divisions in the church even beyond birth control. At a very practical, local level, most of the seminary faculty at St John Vianney signed a letter of dissent along with many US Theologians. It cost them their jobs. The St John Vianney Seminary faculty were virtually wiped out and quickly replaced. Along with the replacements came some suspicion, mistrust in the diocese, and certainly a staff that, of necessity, were going to have to "make it up as they went along", since they had about one month to prepare.

In September 1968, I began major seminary, carrying these treasures of the summer with me.

In some ways beginning major seminary had a bit of a reunion feel to it since our class was now reunited with friends in classes a year or two ahead of us. I found it easy to adjust and to mingle with upper classmates. And found them most welcoming. Because of my voice, and some limited skills in music I was welcomed by the musicians. But there was another group that now appealed to me after my summer of 1968: The Restless Rebels, those slightly unconventional and slightly irreverent guys convinced they were called to change the priesthood, and the church they were to serve, from within.

The seminary itself was in a mode of adjustment; first to many new faculty members, and to Vatican II recommendations, and a general cultural shift of the late 60's and 70's. A search for relevance was encouraged, by some, balancing new ways with tradition. Others were busy bolstering the medieval church battlements against a new age. A traditionally cloistered seminary began opening up. In second year, students were allowed cars on campus and increased off campus freedoms. There was a, healthy as far as I was concerned, push-pull between expanding into the future and a conservation of the past. Heated political discussions, and communal life among those with whom you disagreed became a new normal. While academics remained a central part of life, good studies were assumed, and the emphasis was placed on a more abstract quality, spiritual formation, a conscientious development of critical thinking and spiritual growth, a kind of calisthenics for the soul.

There clearly was a well-established tradition of hand-me-downs in seminary from upper classmates to the next class and classes below. Many of the in-house, day-to-day management jobs were carried out by us all over time. Each of us was groomed by one who came before us to manage certain aspects of light-housekeeping, cleaning of the common areas, of management of the refectory and meals, maintaining the library, management of a prayer schedule, preparing for liturgical celebrations, even organizing the infirmary for medical and dental appointments. All these aspects of communal living were handed down year after year, mostly in a self-selecting way because of the relationships developed from upper classmen to younger classmen.

There was one aspect of this hand-me-down tradition that was not spoken. By the end of first year, many new friendships had developed. Along the way, in first year there was, as in a smoke-filled, dimly lit room, a hazy awareness of special relationships; a closeness of one student usually from the upper class to a student in a class or two below. These relationships were acknowledged, that is, it was not thought unusual to see two guys sharing common pursuits. And it should be said that there were many long-lasting friendships that developed in seminary. But over time, it became clear that some of these couples, were only slightly veiled homosexual relationships active on campus. Keep in mind, as this section develops, that this was a gradual, slowly evolving awareness, not lit by the glare of stage lights but rather like the lifting of the fog.

It is important to keep in mind, that the relationships I am talking about here to follow, were between consenting adults. Given the headlines in today's news about clergy sexual abuse with minors, I feel I must make it clear that these were not pedophilic relationships. The sexual culture I am talking about was subtle, often ignored, prohibited within the dominant church culture, but it was a growing part of the sexual freedom of the larger culture of the 60's and 70's. In an environment which already seemed ill-equipped with role models for emotional expressions, relationship development and interpersonal intimacy, platonic or not so platonic, there was a proverbial elephant in the living room.

By the time, the second year at major seminary rolled around, I was aware of a handful of relationships suspected of being homosexual. I was not shocked, I was curious. My family had not shown any homophobic behaviors that I was aware of. And upon looking back, one or two of my parents' adult friends may well have been gay. In my late teens, upon discovery that one of our childhood friends had "come out", my mother rather candidly asked if he had ever approached me or my brother in a sexual way (he had not). So, the discovery of same sex relationships was not frightening. As far as I knew, in my family, homosexuality was treated much like sexuality in general; it was also not talked about much, as most things sexual were not talked about. I sensed no stigma; homosexuality was just different. However, it was confusing in an environment where celibacy was the expected norm. But like times past, I was open to exploring. Today this might be called "gay-curious" or "bi-curious." At the time I did not have a word for it. But I did have opportunity.

One evening, after a night out on the town, I was crowded in the back seat of a friend's car along with other guys. We had been drinking, true, we were not drunk, at least I know I was not drunk. In the close quarters, the hand of a friend found its way into suggestive territory. I was, and I think he was, surprised at the rather nonchalant way I simply removed his hand. I was not interested. But what that awoke in me was that I could be interested in sex, not with him, not at that time and place — but there was an awakening. We remained friends just not sexual partners. There was also a foursome of us who travelled on a couple of vacations together. We truly enjoyed each other's company but were not sexually active with each other. Years later, I discovered two of the four of us, after ordination, entered life-long, relationships with other men.

And then, it happened.

Frank, (my name for him in this book) was three years ahead of me. He was one of those slightly irreverent rebels. We met through mutual friends. As a group we grew close. It was not unusual for all of us to spend time in each other's room; over a glass of wine and some cheese and fruit while we talked.

These were not exactly "parties," more like discussions, sometimes serious, sometimes just kvetching. One night after a long rehearsal for a musical review that the student body was preparing; a "first ever" theatrical performance for the public, I visited Frank in his room before returning to my own room for the night. I just stopped in to say, "Hi," but I stayed.

After what was some of our usual conversation, Frank, took the initiative for sex, and I surrendered. I was ready and it was wonderful and truly unexplored territory. Yet the sexual details are not the important details here. Yes, I enjoyed the sex and yes, Frank was my first erotic love. What was important was that in this desert-land of limited interpersonal relationships, I had feelings new and wonderful. I also had dilemmas dire and dreadful.

Most of our sex occurred off-campus. I do not remember any further on-campus sexual rendezvous, foreplay yes, sex no. We found ways to be together off campus and took trips that offered a certain amount of anonymity and discretion. This relationship lasted three years; through Frank's ordination to priesthood, and his first two years of priesthood. I was now a part of an underground culture. At first, I justified it, but in the end, the duplicity disturbed me. I could not live with a secret private life. For me, homosexuality was not the sin, it was the lie that was sinful. Frank left priesthood soon after his second year in the parish. He became active in Buffalo's gay community. We kept in touch for a time, but not sexually. And years later, through a newspaper clipping sent by my parents, I learned he died at an early age from unspecified causes, during the height of the AIDS crisis

After Frank left priesthood, I believe that he too felt more comfortable coming out than leading a closeted life. At the time, circumstances allowed me an out from continuing the relationship with Frank, but it was serious examination of conscience and resolve that kept me from entering another homosexual relationship when the situations arose — and arise they did.

As the sexual relationship with Frank came to an end, I grew close to a man, a couple of years younger than me. I briefly considered beginning a sexual relationship, but it did not happen. In the process, I discovered that he was already in a committed same-sex relationship. In another incident, I was invited to spend the weekend at another friend's family cottage. He had been recently ordained and assigned to the country church nearby. I went for the overnight with a few other guys. As the evening wore on and people were assigned or chose sleeping arrangements, I was paired up with our host. This seemed a practical arrangement, not a sexual overture. I liked him, and we had some things in common, but we did not have a sexual relationship. All was OK until late into the might, under the guise of sleep, he came rubbing up against me. Gentle attempts to awake him were unsuccessful or so they seemed unsuccessful. I did not want to be more aggressive in my waking, for fear that I would wake others in the cabin. I stuffed more of the bed covers between us and went to sleep. Next morning, I purposely stayed behind, until I was the last, and told him what I experienced during the night. He claimed to be unaware of his nighttime activity. However, a few months later, I discovered that what I had experienced was a familiar modus operandi, and not everyone resists. I had one additional overture shortly after my ordination, a fellow priest, about six years older than I, offered a souvenir piece of framed stained glass to me as an *objet d'art* from the recently demolished Cathedral. I was interested — in the glass — not in the priest. But that did not stop his advances. I resisted politely and left — end of story.

I give these examples not for the value of titillation, but to illustrate how prevalent this sub-culture was. And perhaps, although not common knowledge spoken in the open, I suspect that there was a lot of communication *sub rosa*. Perhaps my relationship with Frank was better known than I expected, and perhaps that made me more exposed to subsequent advances. Perhaps it was all coincidence. But it was prevalent.

In retrospect, I do not think of my relationship with Frank a mistake, and I am glad for that chapter in my life. I do think that it heightened my awareness and tested the value I placed on integrity, singlemindedness, more to the point of the gospel's "purity of heart." And it helped me better understand that people sometimes make difficult, even dangerous, and compromising choices, in an attempt to reconcile life's apparent contradictions. As it turned out, I accepted celibacy, but its proposed life-enhancing value escaped me. To me celibacy remained a necessary limitation in order to attain a life calling. I was not convinced of the need for celibacy; I was however convinced of the need for integrity.

This homosexual conundrum did not fill every waking moment of life in major seminary. In time I sought a spiritual director as seminary formation recommended. It was in this spiritual direction that I found a second clergy example that would inspire me. Ben was different from Bill Stanton; more introspective, and his direction was more an exercise of appreciative inquiry and waiting. I was never sure that Ben was aware of my past homosexual relationship but he was aware of my struggle with, and my "terms" of accepting celibacy. The difference between these two mentors in my life was a dynamic difference. Learning with Bill was filled with energy and enthusiasm, like improving your skillful parallel turns shushing down the ski slope. My growth with Ben was like spiritual horticulture. He planted seeds and we waited for them to grow.

"Above all, trust in the slow work of God.
We are, quite naturally, impatient in everything
to reach the end without delay,
We should like to skip the intermediate stages.
We are impatient of being on the way
to something unknown, something new.

*And yet it is the law of all progress
that it is made by passing through
some stages of instability,
and that it may take a very long time"*
— Pierre Teilhard de Chardin 1881-1955 in his letter to his cousin, Marguerite

Not everything at major seem was so intense. I think we have earned a break here, gentle reader, for some lighter notes.

In time the strictly academic courses like Scripture Exegesis, Epistemology, Christology, Dogmatic Theology and Church History gave way to a few practicum focused courses. One of these courses, Homiletics, was an attempt to prepare us for future preaching. The professor was affable, with personal mannerisms which made him an easy prey to student mimics. One of our first homiletic assignments was to prepare a five-minute presentation on how to prepare a homily. It was just to give us each a few minutes public speaking standing on our own as we would many times in future sermons. Perhaps the exercise was setting our own baseline from which we could advance later in the course. Most of my classmates took the assignment with serious affect, and briefly expounded on how they would prepare for a homily. I decided to take a comic approach. Dressed in the image of the professor himself, his style a bit of an exaggeration of the usual attire, I proceeded in my best attempt at satire. I identified each item of his meticulous clerical clothing as "necessary" for preparing a homily, with an ironic focus on the superficial. And so, I pointed out, with comic affect and artificial Latin names, how an ample clergy cummerbund with broad fringe, and false sleeves with French cuffs, and impeccably styled cuff links, were a fashionable necessity for the perfect homily. The five-minute piece got the laughs from my classmates that were intended. I was pleased with the presentation. And at the end, after a suitable pause for effect, to hold us all in a bit of suspense, the professor sat back with a well-intoned, "Well, Well, Well!" I think he enjoyed it. In fact, in many years of priesthood, I have used humor to this effect only rarely. It too was well received. But I am aware of how much work it takes to make it come off and not fall flat.

Seminary mischief was not always limited to individual little acts of rebellion. Sometimes there were little acts of group rebellion.

Every year, around the third Sunday of Advent the church celebrates Gaudete Sunday — see the note below.[4] It was customary that the students of Third Year Theology would host a lighthearted celebration. Perhaps today we would call it a "roast" à la the Washington Correspondents Dinner. The time came for our class to organize the celebration. While it was often difficult to arouse full enthusiasm of this class of "individualists" for any united cause, this was an exception. Keep in mind, that by this time, some in the class had been together for eleven years, so we knew how to read each other well. There was an organizing committee, of which I was a member. As it happened our presentation of a plan for the evening got full class commitment. It was a bit of a departure of past gaudeamus celebrations in so far as we were going to rely on talent brought in from the outside. Many in the class, in fact many in the seminary, were familiar with a singer/comedienne at one of Buffalo's well know pubs, Sadie. Sadie was known for her cabaret style songs as she accompanied herself on the piano; sometimes a little risqué but all in good form. Our plan was to create a one-night cabaret in the Seminary refectory. At this time, I was the refectorian, in charge of the refectory, and had easy access to making the changes in scenery needed to accomplish our "cabaret." We enlisted the help of many of my classmates' sisters as waitresses to add to the ambiance. Sadie came and was at her cabaret best. The "girls," all of whom had brothers in the class, played their parts well and we had a rollicking time. Gudeamus it was! Well, until the next morning.

The memo from the faculty was severe. Who was responsible? They would be disciplined, perhaps with dismissal!

Perhaps it was the late-night conga-line sashaying though the refectory guys and girls all in a row, that went too far, but it was all innocent fun. A class meeting was called to discuss how we would respond. It was determined that no one person or no one group would take the fall, we did this as a class, so if they were going to discipline any one it would be the entire class. This was an amazing, and singular, act of solidarity. We stood together. And other than some fierce scolding, nothing more happened but we had indeed made our mark and I think we surprised ourselves.

In general, our curriculum in the last year could have used more practicum. There were no courses on church finance or business administration. Some help on management of small groups or committees would have been useful since these would come to occupy much of a parish priest's time. The church had been educating us academically and to some degree forming us spiritually, our preparation practically for the world in which we were to work, was more limited. While training men destined to serve as secular priests rather than monks,[5] the church had opted for a monastic model of education and formation as the norm. But there was a gradual awakening to this shortfall.

Our fourth year of theology was our last year in seminary and our ordination to the deaconate. As a deacon we would spend an additional year in internship, most of us in parishes "learning the ropes" before ordination to priesthood. In the past, all fourth-year theology students would all be ordained as a class at the cathedral and spend a short period of time in parishes before being ordained as a class to priesthood. For our class, thirteen who had made it this far, there was a departure in order to spend more time in practical internships before priesthood. So, we were ordained deacons as a class but our ordinations to priesthood would occur one by one, each in our home parishes after various lengths of time serving in parishes.

In my last couple of years of seminary, it had become clear to me that I preferred a counseling ministry rather than a traditional parish ministry. One student in the class ahead of us had been allowed to use his internship year in a Clinical Pastoral Education Program (CPE) in New Haven, Connecticut (footnote in next chapter). This was a departure from the norm, and there was growing pressure in the face of an impending shortage of parish-priests, to keep everyone local and to keep everyone one on a track to fill traditional parish-priest vacancies. But I applied and was granted the internship and was set to begin a new adventure in CPE at St. Raphael's Hospital in New Haven.

Don't wait for the stars to align, reach up and rearrange them the way you want...create your own constellation
— Pharrell Williams — American singer, songwriter, record producer.

Notes from Saint John Vianney Years

[1] **Saint John Vianney Seminary** was a glorious tribute to the church's successful vocation campaign of the 1940's and 50's. It was built in the early 60's with a solemn dedication, May 30, 1963, by His Eminence Francis Cardinal Spellman. The spacious 132-acre campus, 20 miles southeast of Buffalo, nicknamed "Burke's Folly" by some at the time, was a thoroughly modern campus fully equipped for its students and faculty. All students and most faculty lived on campus from September to June. The campus consisted of several new purpose-built buildings for classroom education, a resource library, refectory, multilevel recreation hall, chapel(s), auditorium, gymnasium, faculty quarters, administration and six residence buildings for student quarters plus garages and maintenance facilities. The campus in 1968 housed approximately 200 students, near its capacity of about 240. The property also boasted two recreational lakes and tennis courts. Wow, was an understatement!

This grand hope of the 1960's also witnessed the decline and consolidations of the 70's, 80's and beyond. In 1974, the trustees of St. John Vianney Seminary, East Aurora, invited Christ the King Seminary, from Allegany New York, to relocate to its campus. The trustees of Christ the King Seminary accepted the offer, and the move was made in September 1974. In June 1990, the Diocese of Buffalo assumed corporate sponsorship of the Seminary. In February 2020, with 26 students preparing for priesthood (15 for the Diocese of Buffalo) Christ The King Seminary ceased operations in its current form.

[2] Augustine of Hippo (354-430) shaped the development of the Christian Church, sparking controversy and influencing the ideas of theologians through subsequent centuries. Many commentators think that his stormy youth and personal struggles with sexual desire colored his later views on such topics as Original Sin, Lust, and Procreation.

[3] Pope Paul VI issued an encyclical that shook the Catholic Church to its core by declaring that every use of artificial contraceptives is immoral. The document, "Humanae Vitae" ("Of Human Life"), was a shocker because many Catholics had hoped the pope, with the widening availability of the pill after its appearance in 1960, would open the way for Catholics to use birth control. When the encyclical was published on July 25, 1968, the response from Catholic moral theologians was overwhelmingly negative. The opposition of theologians was not just behind closed doors. It was very public in scholarly articles, op-eds, news conferences and signed petitions. Both Catholic and secular media covered the dispute extensively. Disagreements in the Catholic Church over sex made good copy. It is uncertain how many Catholics left the church over this teaching, but it is clear that even more stayed, continued to go to Communion, and simply ignored it. Rather than shoring up the authority of the hierarchy with the laity, "Humanae Vitae" undermined it. In the laity's mind, if the church could be so wrong on this issue, why should they trust the church in other areas? "Humanae Vitae" was not just a dispute about sex. It quickly became a dispute over church authority. — Reese, Thomas. *Humanae Vitae: Sex and Authority in The Catholic Church*. July 20,2018. National Catholic Reporter — And opinion column noting the 50th anniversary of the controversial encyclical of Pope Paul VI

[4] *"Gaudeamus Igitur"* ("So Let Us Rejoice") or just *"Gaudeamus,"* is a popular celebration during the academic year in many European countries. In the university tradition it is a jocular, light-hearted composition that pokes fun at university life and its exhortations to enjoy life. In the Church Tradition Gaudete Sunday is the third Sunday of Advent in the liturgical calendar of the Western Church in which the words of the Introit are "Gaudete in Domino semper: iterum dico, Gaudete." Rejoice in the Lord Always, Again I say rejoice. Gaudete Sunday is a brief burst of enthusiasm that interrupts the more somber patient waiting for the coming of the Christ during the season of Advent.

[5] The term "secular clergy" refers to deacons and priests who are not monastics or members of a religious community. A "diocesan priest" is a Catholic, Anglican, or Eastern Orthodox priest who commits themself to a certain bishop and diocese and is ordained into the service of that diocese (a church administrative region). That includes serving the everyday needs of the people in parishes, but their activities are not limited to that of a parish. *Secular clergy* are ordained deacons and priests, who do not belong to a religious institute or monastic community. While clergy in monastic communities and religious

congregations/institutes take religious vows of chastity, poverty, and obedience and follow the rule of life of the community to which they belong, secular clergy live in the world at large (the secular world). They promise of obedience to their bishop and (in the Roman Church) promise to lead a celibate life. They do not have a promise of poverty.

New Haven

I arrived in New Haven at the beginning of January 1974 having been ordained a deacon and completing my Master of Divinity degree in 1973. A friend who I had met during my last summer working as an orderly accompanied me. We not only had worked together but also shared many a horseback riding summer adventure. I enjoyed her company; to me, it was a platonic relationship. Perhaps my unconscious repression and conscious suppression had been so well ingrained I did not know what her feelings were for me, we were just friends. But as I look back on this moment of my arrival at Saint Raphael's Hospital; newly ordained a deacon and accompanied by a fair maiden, we probably raised a few eyebrows.

I had expressed my interest in Clinical Pastoral Education (CPE)[1] because it was an opportunity to specialize in an area of ministry beyond traditional parish ministry. I wanted to open the door to some form of counseling-related ministry when I returned to the diocese of Buffalo. My CPE experience was to be much more than I had imagined.

Since CPE was organized in twelve-week quarters, I would be joining some in my CPE group who had completed some quarters in advance of my arrival. Members of the CPE groups were to complete four CPE quarters, although we did not all start and end at the same time. We were organized into small groups of six members in each group led by a Certified CPE Supervisor who had completed advanced training in addition to his or her ministry degree. The supervisor of the group I was to join was a Methodist Minister, Bill. Peer members of the group included young clergy of various churches; the United Church of Christ, a Presbyterian, and a Mennonite pastor from Yale divinity school, a Roman Catholic priest from New Zealand, and a young nun from a convent in Wisconsin recently graduated from Marquette. There were two other CPE groups with an equally diverse make up, supervised by two other CPE supervisors. While there were times when all three groups gathered together most of our work was done in small groups, so we got to know each other rather well. The "training ground" so to speak was St. Raphael's Hospital where we would function as hospital chaplains. I lived on the hospital grounds, on the second floor of the CPE center, with two Roman Catholic priests, each with our limited one-room accommodations and bathroom down the hall. Some of the women in the program lived with the nursing order of nuns, also on the hospital grounds. A few students who lived on Yale's campus commuted every day.

The curriculum focused on the practical, the emotional, the psychological and spiritual aspects of ministry, a distinct change from my previous seminary curriculum. In the role of hospital chaplain, each of us were assigned an area or areas of the hospital. It was clear that hospital staff were well aware and welcoming of the chaplain's role. Through various small group learning forums, our acts of ministry, as well as our personal strengths and personal shortcomings were opened to constructive criticism and insight. It was a great learning environment. It was also a tough learning experience, gently invasive to our inner thoughts and fears. At times, through the verbatim exercises, our every word was laid open for examination. Through this small group process, it was inevitable that members would get to know each other "warts-and-all" beyond the limits of the usual social or professional conventions.

And so it was, that I got to know Linda. We spent time together with other members of the CPE group. We spent time together with some of the hospital staff. And we spent time together, just us.

Having my familiar triumvirate of self-control, repression and suppression working like a "well-oiled machine" made me a little dense, oblivious, unaware really, of some interpersonal interactions. Besides my CPE group there was a small group of young professionals in the Hospital Physical Therapy Department that I was attracted to or they to me. They were open to including me into some of their social life, and at times I would join them for a night out after work, for some drinks and dancing. This was a familiar social scene to me because of high-school and early college friendships I shared with my brother and a few summer nights at the local disco. I think that for them they enjoyed someone who was in the church and was a bit like them. And perhaps it was just a little tantalizing to see how far I would enter into their world. We continued socializing, and in time, I asked Linda to come along. Linda and I enjoyed each other's company in a slightly forbidden way, nothing overtly sexual just good fun and some dancing. The PT group was probably more aware of the dangerous territory I was traveling, than I was at the time.

There were also other opportunities for Linda and me to be together initiated by friends from the "convent-side." On occasion I was invited to come along on a group outing or to see a movie. While we were surrounded by her convent friends, we also managed to be together.

And so it goes; perhaps our friends saw the inevitable before I allowed myself to be aware. For me, the waking hour arrived on a spring weekend trip to a reservoir park near New Haven. For those who may have passed us by that day, we were just another young couple in love in the park. But for those who knew us back on the campus, we were tempting fate. There were whispers of caution in the CPE household. Whether the relationship was innocent or not, it would not "look good" for the CPE program or the hospital.

Ah, but what could go wrong?

Perhaps it was the day trip to New York City together, or perhaps we were having too much fun dancing "the bump"[2] when out with the PT group. Perhaps it was bringing Linda home with me to meet my parents during one of the breaks in CPE quarters; but it became clear, even to me, that we were indeed in love.

The duration of our relationship was six months since the end of Linda's CPE was in the summer. Linda arrived at the conclusion that when she returned to her community in Milwaukee, she would begin the process of leaving her order of sisters that she had entered when she was fourteen. I began my internal wrestling in another way. We had a few conversations by telephone as we both struck out into an examination of the direction of our lives.

For my part this involved letting my parents know that I was in conflict. In a rare move of "calling in the calvary" to come to my assistance, my mother convinced my brother and dad to visit me in New Haven. To her credit, she viewed this as a guys' thing. How we would talk about this, none of us knew, since our practice in the area of "guy-talk" was pretty close to zero. But they came and we stumbled through the weekend. My attempts to find something for us to do was another in the now frequent exercise of realizing just how completely different I was from my brother and father. Neither of them enjoyed the trip to the museum to view the Edwin Austin Abbey exhibit that I had found interesting, and even though I chose a symphony concert of lighter classics and Boston Pops[3] that had a lot of activity from the percussion section, my brother finally asked me, "What are you trying to do, torture Dad or bore him to death?" Finally, Dad recommended that we just go get a couple beers, and that was the best idea. In the end, the weekend of bro-bonding was helpful, even if clumsy. Dad probably said the most reassuring thing he could have said. He acknowledged that I was in a position to know better than anyone what would be best for me and he would support whatever decision I made. Convincing my mom, would be his role and he offered to take on the job not knowing where I would land.

I decided, after many quiet tears, and a bit of confiding with my CPE supervisor that I would continue toward ordination. Yes, I loved Linda, but I could not find a way to have both Linda and priesthood.

Linda's story should be a book of its own, with her own history and reasons for her decision. But for now, know that she struck out on her own to set up a new life in Chicago. A small amount of cash, and the use of a car for a couple months was all she had to build her new life, and a lot of determination. But more on this later.

Meeting Linda, falling in love and the struggle toward ordination was indeed an unexpected pivotal set of life experiences of that year of CPE. My decision to "stay the course" was a costly one, emotionally, that I had not planned on.

If we insist on being as sure as is conceivable... we must be content to creep along the ground, and never soar.
— John Henry Newman

The skills developed in ministry were the reason I came to New Haven and I was not disappointed. There were many moments of ministry throughout the year at St. Raphael's. Without the actual daily practice of ministry, I perhaps would have made a different decision, but the call I felt was being exercised and affirmed every day; my heart was in this work as much as my heart was also broken.

Lest you think that all I did in New Haven was socialize and fall in love, I will share one pastoral care story. One of my areas to cover as chaplain included the cardiac unit. There was a patient, Pasqual, in his early 30's, recently married, with a severe heart problem, which was not discovered until after his marriage. I visited often and got to know Pasqual and his wife. Records of some of our conversations were scrutinized by the CPE group and thus the group itself got to know Pasqual. On the surface Pasqual was a blue-collar tough guy, but he was scared. Pasqual was not a deeply religious fellow, but our conversations were deeply "confessional," although he knew that I was a deacon not yet a priest. After a time, his near-death experience brought him a new lease on life and his marriage. He was expecting to be released and a bit of the pressure of impending death was lifted for both him and his wife. And then on the eve before his discharge, he went into cardiac arrest and died, in spite of aggressive intervention. Pasqual was the first person, close to my age, whose death I experienced. He was ready to begin life anew but did not have that chance. My own helplessness in the face of such unfairness required a bit of self-examination and part of that turned into a sermon I preached at his funeral. There were no platitudes, and no pious stories. I spoke only of the grief itself, and the human pain of the moment. It was an exercise in preaching only from where we were, clergy and family together, not of some distant hope or heavenly joy. But somehow it was comforting to the family, that someone was with them, not leading them away to some foreign place or thoughts of some afterlife. It was perhaps my most emotionally invested case study and beyond that an investment in his life and that of his wife. Sometimes it is best just to really BE where we are and to let God be with us, rather than to search for a reason in some distant horizon.

Another set of relationships developed at St. Raphael's, were the ecumenical relationships among the CPE group. My growing-up in a parochial Roman Catholic setting generally left other faiths, even other Christian faiths, somewhere at the outer edge of my experience. Here, in this CPE setting there was a great sense that we shared a common bond. I was surprised and honored when my supervisor Bill, asked if I would like to preach at his Methodist Church one Sunday. I don't know why he asked, and I don't know of any others that were asked. In retrospect I believe that he knew how valuable it would be to stay "in-the-saddle" so to speak until I reached ordination. Perhaps such was his sensitivity to my struggle in the months after Linda left. Bill also preached at my ordination sharing a sermon moment with Bill Stanton.

You are constantly invited to be what you are.
— Ralph Waldo Emerson

Also, in the months following Linda's departure, there was a friend from the larger CPE group that helped ease the way, filling in some of the valleys of despair with humor and leveling mountainous decisions into manageable molehills. Jim McGlone, one of the priests who lived at the CPE center was a character. He was always referred to by his last name, not his first, as if the name itself indicated a unique essence. "McGlone" was a brand of sorts, with a particular baffling and sometimes bizarre but benign style of interaction. Conversations with McGlone, were exercises in listening to a stream of consciousness, often self-effacing; a mysterious loose association in a monologue of late-night comic proportions, or a lecture by Professor Irwin Corey[4]. Somewhere in his labyrinth, I was entertained and supported. McGlone was a delight, slightly irreverent with an occasional sexual innuendo, and a good antidote to self-doubt or false confidence.

As the end of the year approached, more attention was given to my upcoming ordination. Given that I was returning to western New York, either I should be ordained in early December before the snows arrive or wait until spring 1975. As it turned out, I chose a date of 07 December 1974. The coincidence with the anniversary of Pearl Harbor did not escape me, but scheduling turned out to be a logistics problem and so it fell to 07 December. Between my own plans for the celebration, my family's enthusiasm and pride, and Bill Stanton's generous involvement, it turned out to be quite the event.

The Church celebrations involved both the solemn rites of ordination on Saturday evening and the more joyful contemporary celebration of my first mass on Sunday. The public reception and catering were exceptional, and the guest list was large. Beside the expected family and friends, there were many seminary professors attending. I was the last in my class to be ordained that year, so many recently ordained members of my seminary class joined in as well. And new friends from New Haven made the trip to join the celebrations. My parents were diligent in finding accommodations to house several out of town guests.

One guest, just by being present, spoke volumes about the significance of the day in a way that most of my guests could not know. This was no grand accomplishment as twelve years preparation might lead some to believe. This was not the induction into special cultic rituals and mysteries as first seen through the eyes of a fifth grader in his essay. It was a truly humbling acknowledgement of a call, that I had ample opportunity to ignore, but could not. A call to lead people on their spiritual journeys; a call that above all else, I accepted with some fear and trembling.[5] In many ways, I was joining a special group, just not the special group highly visible to most people in the congregation that ordination day. I was yielding to a will greater than my own. I was wondering along with many who had wondered before me, as reluctant leaders, "Surely, Lord you must be calling someone else." I was saying "Amen" and joining the leaders I had read about in Scriptures; who asked, "Why me?" Such a rush of joy and pain, one person could understand like no other.

I had invited Linda to attend, and she accepted. For some this may have seemed incredible, or perhaps even cruel. But there was no other person who knew exactly what was involved in my decision and the cost to both of us. Amid the celebrations we had little time together. In the evening, a few guests gathered at my parents' home for an "after party" party. With most folks celebrating in the family rec-room, we had a chance and stole a private moment. We both came to this day knowing that neither of us could lead a double-life and maintain the relationship in duplicity; although we were both aware of some who did manage a secret life. We understood that the only way for us to maintain integrity was to make this our last moment. And so, we held each other and cried our good-byes.

Linda left to build her new life in Chicago, and I would soon be assigned to Our Lady of Victory Basilica.

"A purely rational man is an abstraction; he is never found in real life.
Every human being is made up at once of his conscious activity and his irrational experiences."

— Mircea Eliade, *The Sacred and the Profane*

Notes from New Haven

[1] **Clinical Pastoral Education** is interfaith professional education for ministry. It brings theological students and ministers of all faiths (pastors, priests, rabbis, imams, and others) into supervised encounter with persons in crisis. Out of an intense involvement with persons in need, and the feedback from peers and teachers, students develop new awareness of themselves as

persons and of the needs of those to whom they minister. From theological reflection on specific human situations, they gain a new understanding of ministry. Within the interdisciplinary team process of helping persons, they develop skills in interpersonal and interprofessional relationships.

[2] The bump was a 1970s fad dance introduced by Johnny Spruce in which the main move is to lightly "bump" hips on every other beat of the music.

[3] The Boston Pops Orchestra performs music of the past and present, appealing to the widest possible audience with a broad spectrum of styles, from jazz to pop, indie rock to big band, film music to the great American songbook, and Broadway to classical, making it the perfect orchestra for people who don't know they like orchestras!

[4] "Professor" Irwin Corey (July 29, 1914 – February 6, 2017) was an American stand-up comic, film actor and activist, often billed as "The World's Foremost Authority." He introduced his unscripted, improvisational style of stand-up comedy at the San Francisco club *the hungry i*. Lenny Bruce described Corey as "one of the most brilliant comedians of all time." For fuller appreciation google *Professor Irwin Corey* and watch a video.

[5] There is a special nuance here of "fear and trembling" borrowed from classic studies of religious symbol and the sacred. The works of Cilliers (regarding Rudolf Otto) and Mircea Eliade, noted in the bibliography give fuller insight if the reader is interested. But briefly here, studies of the sacred, and of religious symbol reveal that there is an inherent dynamic in man, in which man is both attracted to, and pulls back from great power and spiritual enlightenment in life. There is a "push-pull"; we dare to approach God because God dares to approach us. There is something about God that is both awful and awe-filled, overpowering, and empowering. Man is a bit like a moth to the flame.

Our Lady of Victory Basilica

I had no idea where I would be assigned after ordination. In the church, one goes into ordination ordained to serve at the pleasure of the bishop. While one hopes for a mutual meeting of minds, that is not a guarantee. I knew that my expressed preference for a counseling related ministry did not fit the current diocesan plan. My hope for further education in psychology or social work was out of the question and hospital chaplaincies positions were closed at the moment. The diocese needed to fill parish vacancies. The expressed new policy was for each newly ordained priest to spend three years in parish ministry before considering specialized ministry. I accepted that policy with an eye to specializing after three years. The assignment to Our Lady of Victory Basilica was considered a "plum" position by most people. Our Lady of Victory (OLV) was led by a competent experienced clergy with a good reputation. The parish was large enough to have a team of clergy, so there was, perhaps, a chance for some fellowship with the other assistant clergy on staff. The last associate who recently vacated the position I was to fill was known to me and liked by most in the diocese so I had a sense that this was a "good thing" coming my way. Not all my classmates were as lucky; parishes and the pastors who lead them acquire a reputation, and not all were such a gift as OLV.

The church structure itself, was an architectural landmark notable for its status as a basilica;[1] a pre-depression era monument to over-the-top baroque style, OLV basilica seated 1500 on a Sunday and still was able to fill most seats in an era where the decline in attendance was beginning to be noticed. OLV basilica and parish was one part of a sprawling complex founded by the local hero and not-yet-canonized saint, Father Nelson Baker. The complex included a hospital, orphanage, home for unwed mothers, high-school, and grade school. The complex of charity institutions had since been divided into more manageable parts. The parish was but one part. It had remnants of ages past with its multiple masses per day, evening devotions, and scores of shrines within the church itself. But it also had some well working signs of the new age, with active Parish Council members and a Parish Liturgy committee, some contemporary music enjoyed by young people, as well as its ponderous and boisterous Wurlitzer theatre organ played by an aging dame who was an institution herself. All things considered, if I could not pursue my first choice this was a good place to start by fulfilling the three-year mandatory parish ministry.

My welcome at OLV was warm. All three parish priests (later joined by a fourth, resident deacon) met regularly on Mondays to discuss, plan, and divide up the tasks and report to each other their work. I was fortunate to be a part of a reasonably well-working parish staff. Clergy each lived in a small apartment (living room, bedroom, and bathroom) with a common dining room, where meals were served by a cook, and a living room that was never used. The unused living room turned out to be symptomatic of rectory life. Clergy routinely retreated to their own rooms near the end of the day to relax alone. We had a housekeeper, for cleaning and our laundry. There were some holdovers typical of a style of living from ages past, such as the bell on the dining room table to summon the cook from the kitchen when something was needed. There were peculiarities, but all-in-all, this was a positive clergy lifestyle.

Since there were two unused guest bedrooms next to my suite, I eventually commandeered one room for my own office. The other two clergy used the parish secretary and limited church office space, along with a small writing desk in their apartment. I opted for a more efficient "working private office" and provided my own typewriter, printer, and copier, that gave me a private working space and took a load off the parish secretary. We were all different in our work discipline but worked amiably, respecting each other's input. My approach to life and liturgy was perhaps a little to the "left" for the pastor but we got along well. The other assistant held theological and liturgical positions similar to mine but a personal style different to my own. We got along well but lived and worked in different social circles.

With so much going for it, there was one major emptiness. There was little, actually I cannot think of any, interpersonal intimacy. I am not talking sexual intimacy. There was no personal intimacy. No sharing of who we were, how we felt, what excited us, what we worried about. Our talk was all work, or perhaps diocesan news; nothing about ourselves was shared beyond what we were doing. We lived under the same roof, but we did not share a life together. There was, as I came to find words for it, no language of the heart shared among us. This relationship of parish clergy made clear to me what I had first described as the emotional dessert of minor seminary, and barrenness of major seminary. My CPE experience by contrast awakened the richness of a language of the heart but I had now returned to the desert.

Parish life ran without any surprising hitches. Of course, there were "ups and downs" but nothing out of the ordinary. I enjoyed personal relationships with the laity with whom I worked in the parish, but all had some implied set limit; I was their priest, their pastor, these were good people and good working relationships not intimate relationships.

Eventually, I was able to negotiate some time to work in one of the diocesan charities, as a pastoral counselor. I hoped to *parlay* my contacts at Catholic Charities into an eventual part-time counseling ministry or a chance to return to school for a counseling related degree. Also, through a clergy friend I was able to use my CPE credentials to lecture at the University of Buffalo on Death and Dying. Both of these options were in addition to my parish responsibilities. I had the impression I was mapping out my future.

I actively pursued ecumenical relationships. My CPE experience had already primed me to know the value of these relationships. These relationships eventually lead me to the realization that I had more in common in the way I interacted with my ecumenical peers than I did with the persons with whom I lived. One of these ecumenical clergy friends introduced me to a biography of John Henry Newman. I was familiar with John Henry Newman, as a convert from The Anglican Communion (Church of England) to the Roman Catholic Church, and I knew of the Newman Centers on college campuses that ministered to college students. I was aware of his current path to Canonization as a Saint. However, I had come to know of John Henry Newman as a type of Catholic hero, a convert to the true church. The biography and my conversations with my Episcopal clergy friend made Newman's life and his writings more universal, and his eventual conversion to Catholicism more interesting to me. His personal agony and decision making, and twenty some odd years after changing to the Catholic church, his agony once again, over the church's decision to proclaim Papal Infallibility, awakened in me a new appreciation for the relationship between the Anglican Communion and Roman Catholicism. More importantly I saw a fluidity of thought and faith coursing between the two churches once false divisions were minimized or removed.

Keep in mind, gentle reader, there was no grand "light-bulb" moment, this was a gradual exploration of what was developing in me, a newfound kinship not only with the Episcopal clergyman but with a sister church.

Nearing the end of my third year in the parish, I began more actively searching for counseling related opportunities for ministry in the diocese. These included Hospital Chaplaincy but also avenues to pursue an advanced degree which would be recognized in secular institutions. I had, along the way, developed a conviction that I wished to have professional credibility in both the church and in the world. I did not doubt my church education but I wanted to also be credible in the secular world and have that secular language to speak to the people whom I served. For me, that meant dual degrees recognized by both the church and the state. I had become friends with John, a handful of years older than I, who belonged to the same religious congregation as my spiritual director in Seminary.[2] John had followed the path which I was trying to carve out myself; advanced degree (PhD), and full-time work as a marital counselor at Catholic Charities.

During what was to be my last year in parish life, the diocese revised its policy. Now decreeing that it would be at least five years of parish ministry before anyone would be allowed to pursue specialization in ministry. Two more years was not an impossible hurdle, but I could see further into this writing on the wall; this was just a stop-gap policy. I would be swimming up-stream for the foreseeable future. More to the point, there was no one on the sidelines encouraging me, only obstacles placed in front of me.

Clearly, I needed a different strategy. At first, I thought that perhaps getting out of the diocesan structure and into a religious order or a religious congregation such as my friend, would provide more professional freedom. I began my research. Soon my clergy friend, John, moved from Buffalo, New York to San Diego, California, for an opportunity within his Eudist community. Eventually I followed him for a visit to San Diego with the expressed purpose of discussing a change to the Eudists, and an advanced degree, and a counselling ministry.

"You'll get mixed up, of course, as you already know.
You'll get mixed up with many strange birds as you go.
So be sure when you step. Step with care and great tact
and remember that Life's a Great Balancing Act.
Just never forget to be dexterous and deft.
And never mix up your right foot with your left."
— Dr. Seuss, *Oh, The Places You'll Go!*

My world was about to open up before me in an unchartered course.

It was January in Buffalo and a trip to sunny Southern California seemed just the tonic. John invited me to spend a few days with him to explore my plans. The flight to San Diego had a lay-over in Chicago, O'Hare. While waiting at O'Hare, a light went on! I knew that Linda had moved to Chicago, but because we had both been faithful to our promise, I did not know how to reach her and it had been nearly four years since we had spoken. I had time on my hands and with my best Columbo[3] investigation techniques, I bumbled my way to the pay phone (they still had pay phones in 1978) and dialed 411, the number for information. I found Linda's phone number easily enough but thought twice about calling her direct without any advance warning. I continued to attempt to find her address. It took a few calls and a little bit of fabrication but eventually I got the address. Perhaps I could write a letter, send it, and see her upon my return trip. I had already decided to maximize my layover in Chicago on my return trip by staying a few days with friends South of Chicago. I boarded my flight to San Diego with Linda's address in hand. I was missing her postal code but was confident that I could get that later.

While in San Diego, I wrote my letter, casually saying that I was returning through Chicago, could we meet — just this once.

My conversation with John, was as expected; candid, understanding, and unblinkingly honest. Yes, professionally what I was looking for in a specialized ministry would likely be possible with the Eudists, but would life in community with the Eudists answer my desire for intimacy? Not likely. I thanked John for his candor.

On my return trip, I stopped to visit Chicago friends as I had planned. I contacted Linda, and broke our promise of four years, as neither of us had planned. And yes, we would meet.

I had not been to Chicago before, so, Linda took me on a one-day tour, the Art Institute, the Magnificent Mile and lunch at a Chicago institution, Due Pizzeria. I was not equipped for Chicago's January snow, slush, and salt but I hardly noticed. At lunch we both brought each other up to speed on how our new lives were progressing. As it turns out we both put on our best faces; I was truly frustrated and searching for a more fulfilling life, and Linda was making the best of a difficult time and had only recently found her footing for building a new life, but we told each other we were doing fine. At the end of a wonderful day I took the commuter train and returned to my friends' home South of Chicago. I was to return to Buffalo the next day so I called Linda to say good-bye. She was distraught, and told me never, never, to do that again. What for me was the joy and excitement of being together for the day, was for her, so very painful. Again, we parted in tears.

"You will come to a place where the streets are not marked.
Some windows are lighted. but mostly they're darked.
But mostly they're darked.
A place you could sprain both your elbow and chin!
Do you dare to stay out? Do you dare to go in?
How much can you lose? How much can you win?"
— Dr. Seuss, *Oh, the Places You'll Go!*

The return to rectory living, and its detached interpersonal sterility, spurred me on to find a way forward. I knew I could not continue to live a life devoid of sharing that life with someone I loved. It was clear that even the best of rectory situations, was not for me. I began to discuss my dilemma with my episcopal clergy friend, Ed. Through conversations with Ed, and with the added insight of the John Henry Newman biography, I began to ask questions about the possibility of changing churches. I did not doubt my call to priesthood but it was becoming clear that I may be in the wrong church. I could feel the fit immediately. The Episcopal Church not only offered the possibility of married clergy, but it also offered a freedom of expression of ministry in ways that fit me. The Episcopal Church did not offer the security of familiarity or easy financial support during transition, but a door had been opened. I quickly saw that many of my personal, theological, and pastoral positions on church life, fit more mainstream in the Episcopal Church whereas in the Roman Church these same positions placed me a bit out in left field.

As I began this exploration, I began it as if no one had ever made this journey. In fact, many people over the years have made my journey, but at the time it seemed like it had never been done before. Ed put me in touch with some people from the Episcopal Diocese of Western NY who were open to my inquiry and helped me to map out a route.

*"We all live in our own world. But if you look up at the starry sky —
you'll see that all the different worlds up there combine to form constellations,
solar systems, galaxies."*
— Paulo Coelho — Brazilian novelist employs rich symbolism as he depicts spiritual journeys of his characters

I believed that I had found a way! In my excitement, who would I tell and how could I share the news of my discovery? In the span of a few weeks my world had opened wide, frighteningly wide open!

I sat on my new-found freedom for about two weeks. Tossing and turning in my bed at night, sorting out one anticipated problem after another, my concerns were not whether I should pursue this new path, but rather how to pursue this new direction. My underlying feeling was confidence. All of my "figuring-out" was still in my head. I had not shared which way I was inclined; I was still inquiring. Certainly, I had not told my parents or anyone of my Roman Catholic colleagues what my decision was. It was all a bit wobbly. Not wobbly as in uncertain, wobbly as in fragile and new-born, in need of nurture and time to grow a plan.

"The earth's axis wobbles. Life isn't nearly as stable as we want it to be."
— Jodi Picoult, *My Sister's Keeper*

And then, as if I were keeping this new possibility a secret from the most important person, I thought to call Linda. I know, I know, what is it that I don't get about "never again"?

On February 13, I tried to call her and there was no answer. So, with all of the detachments that I had been learning in seminary, I just thought to call her the next day. The next day for most people in love would have registered as Valentine's Day, but for someone who was only beginning to break free of the royal triumvirate of repression, suppression, and self-control, I was oblivious. Her phone rang, she answered. I discovered that, in my excitement, I had not actually planned what I was to say. What came out was, "How would you like to marry an Episcopal priest?" In response to my unorthodox Valentine's Day proposal, Linda simply said, "Yes." Only later did I discover that hers was a strategic response to buy some time. We talked briefly and from then on, we were in touch as I figured my way forward to my future and to Chicago.

During the remaining days of February and the months of March and April, I set in motion my plan. I had little money, maybe two thousand dollars, and no real means to augment that amount quickly. It was clear that while making the change to the Episcopal Church I would essentially be unemployed. And I assumed that such a major change would be better done, with a geographic relocation. It would be an embarrassment for the diocese, and probably for my parents, so best to leave town.

Staff at the Episcopal Diocese of Western New York recommended relocating to the Episcopal Diocese of Chicago, and since Linda was in Chicago that made sense to me. I sought out paid CPE internships; there were two in Chicago. So, I applied. The stars were aligning and pointing to Chicago.

After some of the pragmatics were starting to fall into place, and before any permanent decisions were announced, I decided to take some time for retreat and recollection and perhaps an infusion of spiritual strength. A seven-day Ignatian retreat, located in Des Moines was recommended. The retreat and its location would allow me to make a stop in Chicago for a CPE interview and to see Linda.

I travelled to the retreat center with so many things up in the air. Feeling right about the direction I was heading without really knowing all that it would entail or where I would end up. I also began to realize that I would be leaving so much behind. And this would definitely be a "step-to-far" for my parents and perhaps for some of my friends. Some reassurance would be nice.

The retreat master set the structure for the retreat; scripture choices followed by a lot of quiet and reflection and some writing, along with some processing with him. The days proceeded; the experience was somehow comforting, mostly in being a retreat from the whirl that I was living in at this time. But one moment struck me to the core. The passage at the end of the day, three or four days into the retreat, was from Genesis 22: the story of Abraham's test and the sacrifice of Isaac (Verses 1-19).

Before bed, I reread the passage and my favorite compline prayer,[4] and left my mind open for some insight as to what this might mean for me; nothing.

A storm was brewing, I prepared for bed. As the rumbling and flashes of light rolled in, I crawled under the sheets and just starred to the ceiling. I had many years previous stopped wearing pajamas to bed, so, I was just there, in my birthday-suit; it seemed fitting. In the darkened attic room with a rumbling night sky above, in a strange city, in a strange bed, I felt a little vulnerable, not really frightened just out of place, out of my familiar place. Listening to the storm made me more aware of the power of nature, and nature as a frequent metaphor for the power of God, all-present, strong, awe-inspiring, and sometimes awful. With the clouds bursting above, and lightening affects worthy of a Cecil B. DeMille movie, I decided to get up and read the passage once again; once again nothing. I returned to bed and listened deeply within.[5]

Then it came. Not a literal voice, but clearly a voice in my darkness; "Go with what you know as best, and I'll provide the rest." I fell asleep repeating the mantra-like rhythmic words.

The similarity of my new mantra to my father's advice back in New Haven did not escape me. It also did not lessen the significance. It was, if anything, a confirmation that these words had been trying to find their way into my life for some time. They were no longer to be advice from an outside voice but rather, I must now interiorize them, make them my own. This Scripture passage and mantra have stayed with me ever since.

I returned from retreat with no more money in the bank, and no less problems to resolve, but confident that I was to continue. My interview at the University of Chicago Hospital Chaplaincy program did not result in any immediate assurances. In fact, one of my interviewers (there were three) suggested that perhaps I was using CPE as a crutch during this transition. Actually, she used a Freudian "breast to suck on" analogy which I found a bit of a caricature, but hey, I was sitting in the interviewee's chair, not the interviewer's chair. My response must have been sufficiently confident since I received a confirmation call of approval for the residency a few days later. Things were shaping up, and all roads seemed to lead to Chicago; the Diocese of Western New York recommendation for The Episcopal Diocese of Chicago, the paid CPE residency, and Linda all in one place.

Financially, this move was well beyond a stretch, it was a financial disaster waiting to happen. My paid residency it should be noted, was a grand $6,000 for the year, beginning in September, so I knew I would not be living at the Biltmore. I had about $2000 in savings. And about a $15,000 debt to the Diocese of Buffalo for seminary education. Ah, I bet you are surprised! Yes, seminarians were allowed to attend seminary and defer payment on their "annual loan from the diocese" until they were ordained. Making payments while working the rest of their lives for a modest income. I had begun to make payments to the diocese but I had only begun.

I made an appointment to speak with the bishop. Keep I mind, I had been in seminary for twelve years and aside from the ritual meetings at ordinations to deaconate and priesthood, I had never once met the bishop in person (neither this bishop nor his predecessor). He received me in his office in the chancellery. Without further ado, I said why I had asked for the meeting. I was clear that I was not doubting my vocation to priesthood. I was aware of others who had been in this type of meeting in recent times and they perhaps had asked to be released from their priesthood, this was not my request. In fact, I made no request. I made an announcement. That I would ask for my orders to be recognized by the Episcopal Church. Acknowledging that the Roman Catholic diocese and the Episcopal diocese had a good working relationship, this could be potentially embarrassing, so I assumed to relocate to a different city.

The bishop was calm, nearly flat in expression, but he did share the only personal bit of information I ever received from him. He understood, he said, then shared that his mother was an Episcopalian. With that he stood, I stood, and he said, as a conclusion to the meeting, "You understand that from this moment you are prohibited from exercising any priestly functions in the Roman Catholic Church." Yes, I understood. You may remember, those impediments to exercising priestly ministry from the 1917 code of Canon Law; well, I had just stepped into one of them! The bishop said he would be giving the Pastor at OLV a call as soon as possible. Except for the sharing that his mom was Episcopalian, there were no surprises from this meeting. It was civil, short, more understanding and understated than I expected. I was not looking for help from the bishop, but I found it strange that there was no offer for help, not even a perfunctory "How can I help you?" certainly no severance, no nothing. Even a simple "Thank You" for the work I had done was not possible since he really did not know me or my work. If this detachment were new to me, I might have been bowled over by the apparent lack of concern, but by now I had grown accustomed to the norm.

I returned to the rectory at OLV, and as soon as possible I spoke with the pastor. I really wanted to get to him before the bishop's call, if possible. I did. I know he was not taken by complete surprise; he must have surmised by my sporadic absences in January; to visit San Diego, and by my recent retreat to Des Moines, that something was up; but what? This was just not the surprise he was expecting. In my mind, I was the only person I knew who was making this transition from Roman to Canterbury (I learned this was the phrase used to describe this change from the Roman Catholic Church to the Anglican Communion). But among those in the Roman Church at the time, it was becoming uncomfortably too common for clergy to "leave the church" often meaning that they would ask to renounce the priesthood and become laymen once again, and often to marry. My news was a surprise to him, but he received it graciously. And from him I received an unexpected kindness. He acknowledged that I would no longer be able to function as a priest in the church, but he was quick to follow that up with an offer to stay at the rectory as long as it was necessary to get my feet on the ground in my new journey. It reflected the gentleman that he was. I made it as clear as I could that I had no beef with him or OLV or the other clergy. I had simply found that I could not live out my call to priesthood in the Roman Catholic Church.

My meeting with the bishop on 10 May and the follow-up meeting with the Pastor of OLV would be only the beginning of many more meetings to bring people up to date. My parents had been advised of my plans only a few days before meeting with the bishop. They offered that I return home for a couple months until I left for Chicago. But all planning aside, I awoke on 11 May 1978, my 30th Birthday, unemployed, without a roof over my head, in debt, and the sky at night to guide me.

"And when you're alone there's a very good chance
you'll meet things that scare you right out of your pants
There are some, down the road between hither and yon,
that can scare you so much you won't want to go on."
— Dr. Seuss, Oh, the Places You'll Go!

Before the month of May was ended, I was received as a communicant in the Episcopal Church. This rather basic first step was, for me not a change of faith, but rather a change in the expression of the same faith, now in the Anglican tradition rather than in the Roman tradition. My parents, and two longtime friends of the family who were Episcopalians attended the otherwise private ceremony, with the Episcopal Bishop and the local Rector at Calvary Church, Williamsville, NY. It was a difficult moment for my parents and I am not sure that anyone present really understood the depths of my reasons for changing churches.

Yes, I wanted to marry Linda, and that was not possible, in the Roman Catholic Church. And yes, I was frustrated professionally with being fenced into parish ministry and not being able to pursue a counseling related ministry. Perhaps that is the extent of what my family and friends understood. But there was much more to it. I had, in effect, grown out of the Roman Catholic Church. The Episcopal Church offered broader options; as a church institution it encouraged many of the things that I had grown to appreciate, not only for me personally but as a priest caring for people. Most importantly I had found myself often where I was too far "left" to belong in the Roman Catholic life that was surely solidifying more and more to the right. I was later to describe my inner personal dynamic as "I wanted to be part of a church that had a bigger middle." The Episcopal Church had a greater tolerance for variety in religious practice, and social and moral issues that were important to me. I saw the Episcopal church as having learned to live with diversity; right, left and center, were mutually respected and one could still belong. The Episcopal Church, in my opinion, was more politically transparent, honest, and up-front in living with its conflicts rather than exorcizing those who held differences of opinion on the role of women in the church, homosexuality, birth control and divorce. This made for an outwardly "messy" look; a People of God that reflected God's abundance of variety. It was more of whom I had grown to be.

I also had differences with the Roman Catholic Church in its politics; it was heavily "top down," it was still "monarchial," and some of its positions, such as infallibility and the authority of the church reinforced by Humanae Vitae, were still propping up a medieval structure. I grew tired of justifying my position to the political center or right in the Roman Church, that I had lost confidence in. In pastoral care issues regarding birth control, marriage, death and dying, I clearly fit a broader Episcopal approach than the Roman Catholic approach when counselling people. And in spite of some new language from Vatican II, the Roman Catholic Church was still very much a clergy-centered church rather than raising up the laity in church governance. The very structure of the Episcopal Church's governance gave real power to the laity. The Episcopal Church structure reflected the Ecclesiology I studied in Seminary but was not practiced in the Roman Church. And then there was my growing awareness of the number of clergy who were leading some double life, either in homosexual or heterosexual relationships. I was searching for a church where I could move in from the fringes and belong to a broad middle.

Fortunately, I had anticipated my newly acquired status and made some arrangements to get from the May of my announcement to the September of my beginning at the University of Chicago CPE Chaplaincy. Friends arrived within a few days to move my belongings out of the rectory. For the next four weeks I would return to my childhood bedroom at home. It was a month of planning as best I could for a move to Chicago. A long-time seminary friend offered some furniture from the convent of his parish. The Thonet bentwood chairs he gave me, lived on for another 35 years taking up residence in Chicago, and then again in France before I let go of them. My family offered other basic apartment furnishings and helped to load it into a U-Haul trailer.

Notes from Our Lady of Victory Basilica

[1] A basilica is a church with certain privileges conferred on it by the Pope. Not all churches with "basilica" in their title actually have the ecclesiastical status, which can lead to confusion, since it is also an architectural term for a church-building style. Our Lady of Victory Basilica in Lackawanna, NY (Diocese of Buffalo) is a basilica designated as such by the pope (Pope Pius XI, 1926) and a basilica in architectural style as well.

[2] My spiritual director in Seminary and my clergy friend at Catholic Charities both belonged to the Congregation of Jesus and Mary, more commonly called the Eudists, after their founder St John Eudes. The Congregation of Jesus and Mary was instituted at Caen, in Normandy, France, in 1643 by Jean Eudes, exemplar of the French school of spirituality. The principal works of the Congregation are the education of priests in seminaries and the giving of missions.

[3] **Columbo** or Lieutenant Columbo is the eponymous main character in the successful detective crime drama series *Columbo*. The character is a shrewd but inelegant blue-collar homicide detective whose trademarks include his

shambling manner, rumpled beige raincoat and off-putting, relentless investigative approach.

4. Compline is the last of the daily monastic hours of prayer each day. The English word compline is derived from the Latin *completorium*, as compline is the completion of the working day. From early preparatory seminary days, the prayer of Simeon's Canticle (In Latin – Nunc Dimittis) from Compline, has appealed to me; Now, O Lord, you may dismiss your servant *"Nunc dimittis servum tuum, Domine"*. I had begun familiarizing myself with the version in the Episcopal Church Book of Common Prayer and particularly liked the translation of the 1979 new Prayer Book recently introduced by the National Church; " Lord, you now have set your servant free, to go in peace as you have promised." The added responsorial verses before and after it made for a prayer all of their own; Guide us waking, O Lord and guard us sleeping; that awake we may watch with Christ, and asleep we may rest in peace."

5 "Deep listening" has been a powerful resource in Jesuit spirituality. Deep listening is inspired by the examen prayer developed by St. Ignatius of Loyola (1491-1556). It is the practice of paying attention to ourselves and our relationships and listening for God's presence in our lives so that we respond out of an awareness of God's Spirit in our lives rather than the distractions of ego, fear, or personal blind spots.

Beginning Again, Chicago

The next few weeks in Chicago were a blur; a reunion with Linda, finding an apartment, counting every penny. That Linda would give up her studio apartment and move in with me was a wonderful surprise, and a very practical economic decision. Soon after settling into the new apartment I realized that I had a few weeks free before beginning my CPE chaplaincy. I searched the want-ads and found a short-term job, as a bartender.

Had I ever worked in a restaurant, or tended bar: aside from a friendly family party? No. But this chance to make a little cash to tide me over, did not require any experience, it required stamina. A morning of basic training included how to count change, while keeping the original amount received so as to avoid disputes, how to open-up at the beginning and close-up at the end of the night. I began my job at Lettuce Entertain You the next evening. This was the first year of what was to become a Chicago summer tradition, called ChicagoFest.[1] Lettuce Entertain You, was to have a large bar (a beer tent really) at the main entertainment event area, on Navy Pier in Chicago. Every night some big-name music groups would blast their music into the hot summer night for the 30,000 ticket holders at the main stage and anyone within hearing distance. It was loud enough to be heard at the Wisconsin state line. And hordes of people would cool themselves down with beer after beer. The pace was frenzied, both the beer and the money flowed swiftly. There were times that I would come home late into the night and have nightmares of drowning in beer, being trampled by rolling beer kegs. One night the power went out at the main stage and surrounding area. As some time lapsed, and the power outage delayed the performance, the crowd at the bar grew large and aggressive. It actually felt like those of us on the serving-side were going to be crushed by an onslaught of angry people fueled by alcohol and disappointment. I survived but this was truly a baptism by "the roar of the greasepaint — the smell of the crowd."[2]

After the ChicagoFest event, Rich Melman, chairman of Lettuce Entertainment spoke to me and mentioned that he had heard about my performance during the past two weeks; if ever I was interested in a position in management at Lettuce Entertain You, I should let him know. I thanked him but realized that he did not know where I had come from or where I was headed. Still, the offer was appreciated since we were not exactly flush with cash. Just knowing that I could find a job, was a relief in itself.

As I began my Chaplaincy at the University of Chicago Hospital; we lived far north in Chicago, 52-hundred North, just South of Foster Ave. and Damen Ave. to the west, near the Ravenswood El stop. The Ravenswood neighborhood in 1978 was an affordable neighborhood, clean, considered safe, and not yet gentrified. The U of C Hospital was south; 57-hundred South, the

Hyde Park neighborhood, so the commute was substantial, and in 1978, it was through some parts of town that deserved caution.

In these early months of life together, Linda and I were poor but happy. As I remember it, our first budget was $500 a month; rent, food and utilities, everything really. Linda had only recently stopped her teaching high school classes at Sacred Heart Academy to pursue a PhD in Public Health at the University of Illinois. She had saved some money in order to pursue her PhD, this detour was not in the picture.

My introduction to the Bishop for the Episcopal Diocese of Chicago was reassuring. James Montgomery was helpful to establish that this change, though not an every-day occurrence, had happened before and there were others in the diocese to whom he directed me, to learn from their experiences. He advised me to connect with a married couple who were well regarded in the cathedral parish to help Linda and me navigate some of the common adjustments to Episcopal Church parish life. He put an estimated timeframe on the process and explained some of the possible requirements that would take place over the next two years. All of this was done in a most gentle and welcoming way. This was the beginning of a life-long relationship. Linda and I remained in contact with Bishop Montgomery until his death, some forty-plus years after we first met.

On December 02, 1978 Linda and I were married in the beautiful, yet tiny, Chapel of St Andrew on the grounds of St James Cathedral. Bishop Montgomery presided along with David Harris, the Canon Pastor of the Cathedral, with 25 friends and family attending. The ceremony itself was simple and touching. I played my guitar as I had at many a Sunday service before, but in 1978, it was still a little new for the Episcopal church and I am certain that Bishop Montgomery had not in his many years, had a bride-groom as guitarist. I don't know if my mother's tears were tears of joy or sadness.

The events around our wedding were a mix of feelings; loving, and tense, contentious and complex, supportive, and stormy; it was also literally stormy. Linda's family nearly arrived in Chicago in time for a family get together the night before our wedding but were stuck in a storm about 90 minutes away and hunkered down for the night but promised to make it for the wedding. This snowfall was the beginning of Chicago's notorious winter of 1978-1979 (more on that later). My family: my parents, brother and sister-in-law and grandmother arrived at our tiny apartment carrying not a few tensions from their journey. And by this, I mean their journey to accepting my recent decisions and our impending marriage, not necessarily their travels from western New York to Chicago. My brother informed me that he agreed to be my best-man, just in case anything went wrong in the future I should know that he would be there. It was not exactly the greatest endorsement of the wedding but gives you an insight into what my family was struggling with, while trying to be supportive. My grandmother arrived a little oblivious to our request not to smoke in the apartment, and after she lit-up my father went to the kitchen and retrieved one of our dishes for eating as an ashtray for her cigarette butts. We made it through the evening, but it was not comfortable. My family stayed with our friends on the south side of Chicago who would attend the wedding the next evening. Yes, those same friends with whom I stayed during my January explorations were welcoming and supportive and now clearly in the know about this change in my life.

A young, widowed friend of Linda's loaned us the use of his corporate apartment in one of the nicer parts of town for our reception after the wedding. Linda had previously served as a governess for his two children after the death of his wife and remained friends with the family. On a shoe-string budget we held the reception for our guests at the apartment and after our guests left, we tidied up the apartment and spent our first night there as a married couple. There was no honeymoon, there was no money.

Our families returned to their respective homes the next day and we resumed our lives. I returned to the CPE Chaplaincy at the U of C. A few days after our wedding; I was in the position of "on-call chaplain" for 06 December. This meant an overnight stay in the Chaplaincy offices. The next evening, one of my colleagues relieved me and took the shift. When it was time to go home, I could not find my car. Chaplains were not high enough on the university totem pole to have their own designated parking spot, so, each day I parked in a different spot as the fates allowed. At first, I thought perhaps I had misplaced my car and then I wondered, could the car be stolen? Eventually, I called the campus police and said, "I think that perhaps my car has been stolen." The police asked me to describe the vehicle. "Yep," he said without hesitation, "It's been stolen alright!" In fact, the car had just been reported, still running, abandoned in an alley not far from the hospital. He offered to arrange transportation to the location. I accepted. We found my car at the dead-end of an alley, deep in snow. It had been hot-wired to start it and it had been stripped of its doors and its stereo, and anything that might be able to be fenced. My new-found friend from the campus police advised not to turn it off since we were not sure if we could get it started again. What did I want to do with it? He knew of a repair shop not far away, checked to see if they were still open, and I got into what was left of my car and followed him to the garage. It was dark, it was snowy and the streets were filled with Chicago's salty slush, now all being flicked up by my tires, landing in the beige interior. What I sight!

After the necessary paperwork and contact information, which would allow for follow-up up next day, I was now free to find my way home.

A taxi from the south side to home was not immediately available — and not within my budget. An inquiry of the garage attendant, as to the nearest El station got me the information I needed. I quickly realized that I would be walking through Washington Park on my way to the 55th Street Elevated Station, alone, in the dark, in the cold, and the only white guy in the neighborhood. No other options came to mind but to keep on going! The dark and cold, and a wee tinge of prickle from the hairs standing up on the back of my head, probably made it seem like a longer stretch than it was. But it was truly no "walk in the park!" Because of the heavy snow, there was no traffic, so I walked in the street because I could not find the sidewalk. Finally, one car did come by and stopped; a young couple rolled down the window and revealed a third person in the back seat. They asked where I was headed. I told them. They asked, "Did I want a ride?" With a combination of lone-white-guy-naivete, and brazen hope, I smiled and said, "You aren't gonna mug me or rob me or something are you?" They smiled, I got in, and they dropped me off at the 55th Elevated stop. It was just a bit of south-side hospitality.

It was at least another hour on the EL before I would be home, it was still dark and cold and I was still alone but eventually the elevated commuter train arrived and I kept on keeping on. When I did arrive home and assured Linda that I was all well in spite of the night's adventures. She showed me the table set, and a long-overdue dinner, which she had prepared to celebrate the anniversary of my ordination.

The silver lining to the night's adventures; well, besides the help from total strangers; the campus police, the garage attendant, and my ride through the park, was to be made clearer in the next few days. It snowed and snowed and snowed. It snowed so much that the mayor lost his job in the next election because Chicago could not dig itself out. So bad was the winter of 1978-1979. Cars normally parked on the street were eventually towed to huge makeshift lots to be claimed by their owners months later when spring arrived. The irony of the situation was manifold; but my car was safe inside at the repair shop during one of Chicago's worst winters in history.[3]

For the rest of that winter I would take the Elevated. The journey was long even on a good day but often made extremely long because of the weather. There were a few days where it took me so long to get to work, that I only had a couple hours before I needed to think about making the return trip.

The CPE residency at the U of C Hospitals was a valuable experience in many ways. The Chaplaincy program was well respected within the hospital and the department had a hand in developing a hospital rape victim's protocol which included involvement of the Chaplain whenever a rape victim came to the emergency room. Besides learning effective crisis intervention methods, it also placed me in a setting to value the work of the police officers, and the ER staff.

A lot could go well, and a lot could go to hell, depending on just how well everyone worked together. The Chaplaincy work also prompted me to explore my next steps differently. I had assumed to return to school to work on a PhD in psychology but through this experience I discerned that my heart was more into a combination of social work and psychology, I was much more a hands-on clinician and I enjoyed working with the multiple facets in a social network for recovery rather than what I perceived was a single focus on the patient alone. As the year's residency drew to a close, I applied to schools of Social Work. I was accepted at Loyola University. A nominal student loan and help from Linda made it work. Loyola's school of social work was located in a posh part of town, and near the Episcopal Cathedral of St James. My commute would be cut in half.

In time Linda shifted gears to apply for a position as director of a Wellness Program at a near suburban hospital. And I would take a part-time job as a mental health technician at Ravenswood hospital, only a few blocks away from our apartment. These moves were a second stage, broadening our life in Chicago as a couple. Somewhere along these early years, the diocese of Buffalo decided to take a more aggressive approach to being repaid for the education loans. I had paid a part but still had more than $10,000 in balance. One of Linda's gifts to me was for her to pay off the balance. Irony aside, my wife paying off my seminary loan, it was a relief to be free of those little postal reminders of a past life.

During two years of grad school at Loyola, I worked weekends at Ravenswood in the In-patient Psyche Ward, usually on the night shift. At Ravenswood I would meet a few unusual characters, not all of them patients. And I would meet one or two folks who would become life-long friends. It was also at this time that, step by step, the process of recognizing my priesthood by the Episcopal Church would progress.

In the Episcopal Church it was clear that I would not be starting from the beginning. My seminary degrees and my ordination would be recognized. However, it was recommended that I take a few courses at Seabury Western Divinity School at Northwestern University north of Chicago. This was to provide some acculturation to the Anglican ways of the Episcopal Church and some academic contacts. Typically, one of the first questions asked of clergy during customary social introductions was often "Where did you go to school?" I soon realized that my answer was too long and perhaps "Too Much Information" for an ice-breaker conversation over cocktails. But I did find the church history classes on the Reformation Period and the 19th century Oxford Movement gave me valuable vocabulary and historical context to make social small talk that my previous seminary education from the Roman perspective, could not provide. Eventually, I relaxed into this social scene, and found that my previous education, and degrees served me well. In general, the two-year period of recognizing my Holy Orders was geared to making me fluent in the language and culture of my new surroundings. I was appreciative. There were, in addition to the educational components, some social and psychological evaluations; weekend "retreats," where all applicants for ministry or prospective candidates for ordination, (and sometimes their spouses) were evaluated, and otherwise scrutinized for suitability. Some steps in this part of the process had the reputation for being overly critical, too analytical, and not very supportive. In time I could see that the candidates' anxieties about the process were valid, although I experienced no problems myself. In later years, I was happy to be asked to use my skills to be part of re-vamping of the diocesan system. Just one area where, in the Episcopal Church, I was drawn into the center rather than placed on the outskirts.

My studies at Loyola, along with required field work, and the formal recognition of my priesthood developed simultaneously. It was determined that I should take the General Ordination Exams (GOEs) as was the norm for all divinity students. Every January, candidates for the priesthood in the Episcopal Church take national General Ordination Exams (GOEs), required for ordination. This is a rigorous week-long marathon of open-book written essays, and closed-book examinations and essays, testing the candidate's knowledge in areas such as scripture, church history, church practices in governance, and pastoral care. There are six defined areas of testing, and each student's work is reviewed by a national board of examiners. Frankly, I was concerned. I was being tested with a group of freshly minted theology students and my seminary academics were more than five years old. My areas of pastoral care were probably more developed than theirs and I probably had an edge as to the integration of the separate areas of study, but could I still pull the necessary five major points of this document, and the six major accomplishments of that out of my hat? I passed all six defined areas (not everyone does – there are re-takes for failed areas). One unexpected personal benefit to taking the exam was that my education in a different seminary system held up well, and in spite of the five+ years since my seminary days, I was able to meet the same challenge as the others. This feeling of competence was a relief and a welcome verification of belonging.

In the end, I would be received as a priest in the Episcopal Church in the fall of 1980 and I received my MSW from Loyola in the spring of 1981. All this while working a part-time job at Ravenswood Hospital on weekends.

Will the future ever arrive? ... Should we continue to look upwards?
Is the light we can see in the sky one of those which will presently be extinguished?

The ideal is terrifying to behold, lost as it is in the depths, small, isolated,
a pin-point, brilliant but threatened on all sides by the dark forces that surround it,
nevertheless, no more in danger than a star in the jaws of the clouds
— Victor Hugo, *Les Misérables*

In my second year at Loyola, our course on statistics required a research project that included the use of certain statistical tools and data analysis. My field advisor recommended that I approach Father Robert Taylor at the Episcopal Diocese. Marion, my field education supervisor happened to be friends with Fr Taylor's family and knew well that he was introducing a new program for the Diocese. Bob Taylor was also completing his advanced degree at the University of Chicago. Marion's recommendation not only was just right for putting me on the right track for my research project, but it also opened up a whole new area in my personal and professional life! I made a proposal for a program evaluation of the Episcopal Diocese's Office of Pastoral Care. Bob Taylor and the diocese were more than happy to take advantage of my offer. As it turns out, I created the parameters for the evaluation, did the data collection and wrote up the evaluation of the Office of Pastoral Care as a student. Bob then hired me to work with him as a colleague shortly after my graduation, in the newly developed service for clergy and lay employees of the diocese. This was the beginning of a wonderful, sometimes complicated relationship with a mentor and colleague in the Episcopal Church. Over the years to come both Linda and I would get to know Bob and his wife, Carvel; professionally great assets and a part of our new Chicago "family."

It was during my classes and field work at Loyola that my focus on clinical work became clearer. I had two field work experiences while pursuing my MSW at Loyola. In my first year I was assigned to assist in the in-patient psyche unit at North Chicago Veterans Hospital, and in my second year I was assigned to a local Community Mental Health Center. What I discovered about myself was that, as eager as I was to help people, I learned just how impossible success for them was going to be if they did not have a system of support. Poverty or near poverty, unemployment, lack of access to medication and physical medical care, and broken family systems all contributed to the level of difficulty for recovery regardless of the underlying mental state of the client, or the clients own desire to be well.

I discovered that it was best for me to work with clients who had at least some of the benefits of a supportive system for their recovery. I was competent and enthusiastic but I learned that I needed to work where the chances of the client's success were greater, because they had the resources necessary for success. Life was difficult enough, even for people with social resources, a job, a certain level of financial security, family support, and access to medical care. This insight led me to explore an area called Employee Assistance Programs (EAP). And that was exactly what the Office of Pastoral Care was, an EAP for Church employees and their families.[4]

By 1981 Linda and I were well on our way from the beginnings of our new life and into becoming an established part of that which we had dared to dream. Linda was well appreciated in her position in the Wellness Program at Skokie

Valley Hospital and would soon accept a new position as Director of a Work-Place Wellness program at Mercy Hospital in Chicago. I began what would be a lifelong relationship with Bob Taylor and Carvel Taylor. I had found my niche in the Diocese working on the Bishop's staff in the Office of Pastoral Care in the professional field of EAP that I desired.

"Don't be satisfied with stories, how things have gone with others.
Unfold your own myth"
— Mevlâna Jalâluddîn Rumi — born 1207 in Balkh in what is today Afghanistan

Notes from Beginning Again, Chicago

[1] **ChicagoFest** was a Chicago music festival established in 1978 by Mayor Michael Bilandic. It was a two-week event held annually at Navy Pier that featured sixteen separate stages, each sponsored by a national retail brand and a media sponsor compatible to the stage's format. In addition to its 30,000 seat Main Stage, ChicagoFest featured 16 other stage areas that seated 2,500 to 5,000, presenting nationally known recording artists. **Lettuce Entertain You Enterprises,** a restaurant group comprising 120 or more restaurants mainly located in the Chicago metropolitan area, was founded by Rich Melman and Jerry A. Orzoff in 1971.

[2] **The Roar of the Greasepaint the Smell of the Crowd** — a mid-1960s musical — is ultimately a story of hope. In the aftermath of an event that has upended society, an absurd union is formed. A band of survivors creates their own new world. Ultimately, this scrappy, eccentric group of survivors find hope from the unlikeliest of sources.... each other.

[3] **Chicago's worst winter** on record at the time: 1978-79. That early December snowfall was the opening shot of a nearly continuous barrage of snow and cold in a landmark winter that would become Chicago's snowiest (89.7 inches) and second coldest (18.4 degrees) on record (the coldest was 18.3 degrees in 1903-04)

[4] **An Employee Assistance Program (EAP)** is a voluntary, program based in the workplace that offers free and confidential assessments, diagnoses, short-term counseling, referrals for treatment, and follow-up services to employees who have personal or work-related problems. EAPs address a broad and complex body of issues affecting mental and emotional well-being, alcohol and other substance abuse, stress, grief, family problems, and psychological disorders. EAP counselors also work in a consultative role with work-place managers and supervisors to address employee and organizational challenges. Many EAPs are active in helping organizations prevent and cope with

workplace violence, recovery from workplace trauma, and other emergency response situations.

Chicago, Love and Care Years [1]

For this chapter, I am reminded of Erik Erikson's stages of psycho-social development. We were, as it turns out, according to his view of human development, right on track, in spite of each of us having taken, what some may regard as a grand detour into religious life. To me this was a sign of an overall unified world; the greater cosmos all works together. We will get to wherever it is we are going, even if "where we are going" is, at times, not where we think we were going. It was as if by some power greater than ourselves, we had squarely landed in Chicago and our life-garden was blooming with Love and Care; to be cultivated during these next twenty plus years of life.

In general, the next twenty years in Chicago were spent working. But that work-life brought us friends and a social life, as well as good incomes. I now look back from retirement to these years and see that they were intensely long hours for both of us. But at the time, it just seemed like that was life. It would not be until we reached our 50's that we began to look for some different way of living. Yes, it was stressful, but that seemed normal. Yes, vacations were short and not too frequent but that too was normal. We enjoyed our productivity. We saw ourselves as fortunate, appreciated and contributing to the world in which we lived.

In an overview for this period of life it becomes more difficult to separate Linda's life from my life. We were a team. Early on in our marriage we came to the decision that we would not have children. Initially we gave the choice for childrearing a few years to rumble around in our heads and hearts. But in the end, we opted to make our contributions more broadly and to express our creative energies without children. We have had several moments in our adult lives where we have enjoyed that decision. Our intimate life and sex life were good, a comfort, and fun, but no children. We each saw ourselves reflected in our work, and that was good. We were both fortunate to have work lives that we loved and which were opportunities for growth. As the years passed, we also discovered a mutual interest in creating living spaces that carefully reflected who we were and what was important to us. Gracious hospitality was also a part of who we were. The renovations of our homes over the years hold many a tale of their own. Only the renovation of our property in France got its own book detailing that four-year project.[2] But there were other renovations, other personal expressions of grace and tranquility that, preceded it and followed it.

My work with Bob Taylor at the Episcopal Diocese, Office of Pastoral Care was satisfying in many ways; it was the counseling related ministry I had envisioned since seminary, it was supported and encouraged by the diocese, and it required both the church and secular credentials. As a matter of fact, being credentialed properly became a necessary professional pastime. Each area of specialization required a set of continuing education requirements, for maintaining professional licenses and credibility. The National Association of Social Workers required certain credentials, as did the License from the State of Illinois as a psychotherapist. Specialized work required being credentialed as an Alcohol and Substance Abuse Counselor, and as an Employee Assistance Professional. Eventually, near the end of my career, there was an additional credential, as a Disability Management Specialist in Mental Health Disabilities. Yes, it was a burden at times but generally worth it. The credentialing processes were also a way to grow a network of like-minded professionals striving for excellence in their field. And it was through these networks that I moved freely to work in the Employee Assistance Professional field to work beyond the Diocese with Parkside Medical Services, Arthur Andersen & Co, and lastly with Northern Trust Co. Each were great companies with professional challenges and opportunities. All of this happened while maintaining my relationship with the Episcopal Church, as a priest, and consultant to bishops, and priests and laity in their congregations.

Perhaps a few tales from this part of my journey would help flesh-out some of these twenty-plus years.

Within a few months after I joined the Office of Pastoral Care at the diocese, there was a parish situation that Bob Taylor was working on. I was aware of it in detail since we shared the clinical aspects of the cases as needed. Bob and I also routinely met with an outside consultant weekly to discuss clinical matters. As it turned out Bob was going out of town and asked me to watch over the case. The bishop was already in the case-loop with the parish priest's consent, but there was the possibility that clergy might play one part of the team against the other; specifically it had been known that the bishop might be manipulated into some soft-hearted gesture when a tough-love therapeutic decision was needed. As it turned out this is exactly what happened. But a tribute to the bishop having listened to Bob's advice, he called me at home. I walked him through what needed to be done to reinforce the therapy plans we had all discussed. He took my counsel and followed the advice. After I was certain that the necessary steps had been taken and all was back on course, I called the bishop. He was a little puzzled as to why I might be calling now that everything seemed back on track. I said that I was just checking to see how he was, since he had a difficult call to make, and made it. He was gracious in his thank you to me for my concern. Days later he expressed his sentiment again, noting that in all his years of ministry, that was the first time someone had inquired about his welfare, when making a difficult decision.

Much of the work of the Office of Pastoral Care was protected by the confidentiality statutes for mental health. So, it is difficult for me to relate the details of the case which brought this all about, but I hope that I have been successful with this as an illustration of the appreciative working relationship that I had with this bishop, and the diocese, and the bishop's next two successors. This was the shared working relationship that was so absent in the Roman Church.

It was about 30 years later when I was in a difficult parish conflict, making some tough calls myself, when such a favor was returned to me by a kind and a compassionate parishioner, and the bishop whom I served. Such ministry to the minister does happen, but not too often.

I thrived in my work with the Office of Pastoral Care. Bob Taylor and I both liked the detective work related to the Employee Assistance Program's fundamental work of diagnosis. In the field of Employee Assistance Programs there is a need for an expertise in Alcohol and Drug abuse treatment. Bob Taylor was helpful in impressing upon me the need for professional certification in this area, and I followed his advice. Working with alcoholics and substance abusers, on the road to recovery, or helping them get on the road to recovery has been one of the most rewarding and humbling professional and personal gifts to my life. There were many a story of clients presenting one or another personal problem in their initial diagnostic meeting; marital problems, some elaborate medical problems, a complex history of family and childhood problems etc., etc., but the skill to wade through it all to "rule-in" or "rule-out" an alcohol or drug problem was essential to the work of the Office Of Pastoral Care; and then determining the steps to help people see their way to treatment and aftercare. Not only did I find the work professionally rewarding, the recovering alcoholics', Serenity Prayer has been my prayer for more than 40 years.

It was also during this time that, on occasion, I would be called upon to help congregations as a group, or a vestry (the lay governing board) within a congregation. The story I am about to tell is not typical of my work with congregations, but it is notable for its expediency. This turned out to be a "right-on" intuitive response, that in the years before Chicago I would not have risked. One's personal confidence can be a great help to others as well as to oneself.

There was a parish in one of Chicago's old neighborhoods; once a place of gentrified living, it had passed through its decline and now was being gentrified once again. The church had shared the neighborhood's ups and downs; its past of faded glory was once again being refreshed. But with this new future there were new tensions between the rector and the lay governing board. The rector had a generally good reputation and had brought the parish through some rough times. But some serious differences with the board (the vestry) had brought out some counter-productive shouting matches between the rector and key lay leadership. In meeting with the vestry and with the rector both separately and together, it became clear that while the differences were serious, they were clearly workable to a solution, and there had been a good foundation in the past. Toward the end of these meetings both sides looked to me for an estimate of time and money needed to resolve their issues. Of course, time and money were not the prevailing variables necessary to finding a joint solution. They needed to better listen to each other; to stop reacting and start listening. I was tempted to put their recovery in this context using accepted conflict resolution strategies. I decided instead, to take a more unconventional tact. Rather than outlining the usual norms and parameters of conflict resolution, I decided to respond literally to their request in terms of time and money. I gave them a general outline of the time for recovery based on research studies, multiplied by the cost of consultations with them for many months. With the dollar signs flashing in front of them, I held out a simple alternative, in the form of an exercise that they could do together in the next week, to reestablish their working together with only minimal oversight by me. The rector and the senior warden (lay leader) were to report to me by phone. My only requirement was that they remind themselves each day in the next week of the amount of time and money it could cost them; and ask themselves how they wished to spend their time and money. At the end of the week, both rector and vestry agreed that they could work toward joint resolutions on their own, at less cost and in less time. I would check back with them quarterly for one year, to see how they were progressing on their own. It was a success; the rector expressed his appreciation over a long-standing friendship well into his retirement years. The congregation managed through the problem with their rector and were pleased with themselves at the money they had saved the parish. An unconventional success, but success, nonetheless. I mention this experience since it begins to show that the supportive relationship in the Episcopal church had freed up my own creativity; in this case creative problem solving. In this environment, I would be more likely to exercise my primitive intuitive and curious self.

"When you hear hoofbeats, think of horses before zebras."[3]
— Medical aphorism coined in 1940s by Theodore Woodward modified here as quoted by Harley S. Smyth

Not all episodes were as successful and some were downright painful. Over many years with the diocese, seven years on the bishops' staff and another twelve as an outside consultant, I worked with several parishes. Often these were cases of long-standing unresolved problems and I was a last-ditch effort. A unique historically black parish in one of the northern suburbs had a series of misfortunes. My work with them in the mid-1990s was indeed a challenge for them and for me but there was good faith on both sides. Nearly all of the parishioners were Black, much of the tensions were around differences between Caribbean Blacks and African American Blacks. They needed a consultant different from me, but I was "it." I wish I could say that I was the miracle-worker they needed but I did serve as a bridge to a future that was a few short years away, yet not available to them at the time. Eventually help arrived in the form of a Nigerian American lay woman at the cathedral and a Nigerian Anglican clergyman new to the Chicago area in 1998. A healthy connection was made, and with cathedral and diocesan support, the parish is alive and well today

At another time I was asked by the diocese to help a church with a long history of conflict; St Alban's (its name for the purposes of this book). This parish had a history of "eating up clergy" (and clergy families). It would be this congregation-type that would be described through clinical anecdotes, in Dennis R. Maynard's book *When Sheep Attack*. Embedded anger in the leadership was palpable. After 18 months serving in combined positions of interim clergy and consultant, I was for the first time in my ministry, accused of incompetence, mismanagement, and the same inadequacies as those who had been gobbled up before me. Fortunately, I had a reputation that countered the fabricated justifications for insisting on my removal. In fact, I had gotten too close to be identifying the source of the problem and a plan of resolution, and they needed to remove me so that they could continue their familiar dysfunction. Since this was not their decision to make, the bishop could have insisted that I stay, however in the grand scheme of things we decided that he would grant their wish. The congregation, with no further targets for their anger, turned upon itself, and sadly closed its doors within the year

In situations like the two churches above, my interactions were unique to them because, as bi-vocational clergy,[4] I was already gainfully employed in another field, and the tensions and detrimental dynamics of the parish did not affect my abilities to earn a living or provide a roof over my head. I was financially independent from their destructive behaviors. In most traditional positions of parish clergy, clergy find themselves in horribly compromising positions, with their livelihood threatened because the parish in conflict is the parish, they serve

I include these two stories of limited or no success to demonstrate that my years serving the diocese were personally and professional fulfilling but not necessarily easy. With the support of colleagues and the bishops themselves, it was a wonderful place to work. I was living my dream — well, most of it.

After about seven years working with Bob Taylor in the Office of Pastoral Care, a surprise opportunity opened up. Bob's wife, Carvel also worked in the EAP field. She had recently left United Airlines EAP and in her new position with Parkside Medical Services, she was looking for someone to manage the EAP for Arthur Andersen & Co. We routinely networked on EAP resources with other EAP professionals, and so, were discussing the position. When Carvel first asked if I knew of anyone that I thought would fit for the position,

I agreed to think about it; that is, think about who, among my peers, I might know to fill such a position. After an overnight think, I discussed my thoughts with Bob Taylor the next morning. I told him that "I would like to be considered for the position." And thus, began what we congenially referred to as "The Custody Battle" between Bob and Carvel Taylor.

To be clear I was not unhappy about where I was, working with the Episcopal Diocese, but I was tempted to exercise my skill in the secular, corporate world. The Arthur Andersen & Co contract was a high-profile, prestigious position. It was also the largest account in Chicago held by Parkside Medical Services. In time, this position working with Andersen's Chicago office, would open for me the management of the entire Arthur Andersen & Co. offices in both Andersen's Accounting and Consultation offices.[5] I interviewed for the position with Carvel Taylor, and with the person who currently held the Andersen World-wide EAP management position. I got the position!

I maintained my relationship with both Bob and Carvel through many professional twists and turns. I maintained my relationship with the Episcopal Diocese of Chicago. This was a glorious time for me personally and professionally feeling challenged and stretched and eager for more.

I was offered the management of the Anderson World-wide contract after a couple years. This meant either maintaining or establishing new EAP services for Arthur Andersen & Co in all of its locations in the USA, UK, and Canada. Around year five of my work with Parkside Medical Services and Arthur Andersen & Co., Parkside Medical Services had a major shakeup in their upper management. There were some corporate power struggles to be sure and eventually some changes that made me question newly introduced procedures. I was directed by the new corporate management to "Make the Elephant Dance,"[6] meaning, I was to implement these new corporate changes in direction and convince the client corporation to like it. Until now services were driven by the client's priorities, and Parkside Medical Services, in order to get the contract, would do handstands if necessary, to deliver what the client wanted. This new approach was a reversal of the terms under which the services had been originally promised.

"Elephant and Mouse were best friends. One day Elephant said, 'Mouse, let's have a party!' Animals gathered from far and near. They ate. They drank. They sang. And they danced. And nobody celebrated more and danced harder than Elephant. After the party was over, Elephant exclaimed, 'Mouse, did you ever go to a better party? What a blast!'

But Mouse did not answer.

'Mouse, where are you?' Elephant called. He looked around for his friend, and then shrank back in horror. There at Elephant's feet lay Mouse. His little body was ground into the earth. He had been smashed by the big feet of his exuberant friend, Elephant."

— Dr. Miriam Adeney, author, associate professor of World Christian Studies, Seattle Pacific University

To make a long story of corporate intrigue short(er), I eventually had to decide to manage the Arthur Andersen & Co account in the way new management desired or leave. Others were also feeling the effects of the shifts made in upper management and I joined a flow of exits. Carvel, for her own reasons, left Parkside about six-months prior to my exit. In my resignation, the reason I gave for resigning was, that with the new changes in corporate direction, I could no longer manage the Employee Assistance Program as Parkside Medical Services desired, and deliver the quality of services that the client, Arthur Andersen & Co expected. This decision was a heartbreaker but staying would have meant making a compromise that I was not willing to make.

Welcome the darkness, embrace it as a canopy from which the stars can hang.

For there are always stars, when we are where we ought to be, amongst the faces we love best. Each with our place, each with our purpose, as fixed and familiar as the constellations. The Darkness is beautiful. For how else we can shine.
— Season 9 *Call the Midwife*, Episode 8

By now I had established myself well enough with my professional peer group that I could consider setting up a private practice. It was a big risk, but people who knew me responded well and had a hand in filling my private practice with clients. Colleagues stepped forward with offers for office space at a good price, as well as referrals of clients and I was able to set up a private practice in downtown Chicago not far from Arthur Andersen & Co, in the heart of the banking district. Even my temporary successor in managing the EAP account referred clients from Andersen to me, such was the quality of relationships and the collegiality established. Although the transition was going well, at times I could not help but think I had made myself unemployed rather than self-employed.

These years were filled with professional development and work-stress, to be sure. But Linda and I had plans of our own. At some point in the mid-1980s we discovered that with all of the social and cultural opportunities available to us, living in a big city, we were not making much use of them. On rare occasion we would take in some theater, a museum, or the symphony but we discovered that our primary source of "recreation" was renovation. By now we were on our third home; having lived in two condos and an 1880's single family Victorian home. Each time we set about renovations of the properties. At first these were cosmetic interior design changes in the condominiums but eventually we reached for the stars taking on an extensive renovation of our Queen Anne Victorian home in the Edgewater neighborhood. This renovation was down to the very bones of the house and lasted four years. During this time, we continued our full-time work-lives.

A scene of domestic bliss from this period might look like this. Well, it actually did look like this: For a time, we found ourselves technically owning a large four bedroom three-and-a-half-bathroom Victorian home, but actually living in one semi-organized bedroom and a kitchen under major renovation and sheets of plastic. There was so much plaster dust everywhere, that on workday mornings I would get up, shave and shower down the hall, get dressed and roll up the cuffs of my trousers until I was safely out of the house, at which point I would roll down the cuffs and proceed to the elevated commuter train in the guise of a normal city-dwelling professional. At another time during the renovations, Linda decided that the multilayers of paint on the sandstone fireplace in our someday-it-would-be-a-dining-room, needed to be sand-blasted away (simple paint stripper did not work). Sealed off with plastic and well masked, Linda sandblasted the fireplace back to its original beauty, while 700 pounds of white silica sand accumulated on the dining-room floor. We discovered eventually that our pet cat thought it was his litterbox deluxe! Ewe! Four years of renovation later, we had a restored gem that we enjoyed for the next 10 years.

"You gain strength, courage, and confidence by every experience in which you really stop to look fear in the face.
You must do the thing which you think you cannot do."
— Eleanor Roosevelt

Linda made a couple of career changes during this time, but it is best for her to tell those stories more fully in her own way. From her management position at Mercy Hospital, she decided that she wanted a job that provided some more immediate gratification. An annual review and departmental report were not sufficient trade-offs for the work stress. Her personal preference would be to trade in her two graduate degrees and her departmental management position, to learn a hands-on trade such as carpentry. The Sunbow Foundation was founded to teach poor minority women the construction trades. The foundation saw in her a great deal for a different kind of trade, a trade-off. Linda was to teach basic math to the Sunbow women. And in exchange she would be able to avail herself of any of the construction trade classes and staff expertise along with a nominal salary. This was a financial cut but a real advantage to our renovation interests. After our completed renovations, and with the closing of The Sunbow Foundation, Linda became a licensed realtor and broker, with residential sales in the top tier of Chicago realtors.

I give this all-to-brief history of Linda's career moves to say that there was a lot going on in our lives in the 80's and 90's in Chicago. And with our work lives, renovation of our homes, and church lives, we gathered an interesting cadre of friends and associates that filled our lives. Many of those friends remain in our lives yet today.

While working full time to develop my newly established private practice, I also did some consulting with the Diocese of Chicago and EAP consulting with Northern Trust Company. Northern Trust had a reputation of being a bank for "old money" and Wealth Management Services. Its corporate profile was an easy match for my experience with Arthur Andersen & Co. Northern was one of the last big corporations that did not have an EAP. Northern had been courted for many years, unsuccessfully, by Parkside Medical Services hoping to win the contract. Little by little, Northern grew more and more comfortable with me. First, one or two individual cases, then a meeting with Human Resources, and at last discussions about "Would I be interested in coming on board to develop and direct a Northern Trust EAP?" Beginning in 1991, I created Northern Trust's Family Assistance Program. The change in name from Employee Assistance program to Family Assistance Program was to reflect Northern's new Human Resource's Family focus, it was in fact, an EAP with a bit more marketing to family. It was with Northern Trust that I spent the last nine years of my work life before retirement. This was a great opportunity. I was able to set up a new program having learned from past errors (mine and others) along the way. Senior management above me, knew of my clergy background and knew of my previous EAP history. This all seemed to make me all the more desirable candidate. I had a happy, yet stressful, nine years at Northern. I was creating my own EAP baby! When fully developed, Northern Trust Family Assistance Program covered all employees and family members across Northern Trust's 55 office locations in the USA, and offices in Canada and the UK.

My work years at Northern Trust were in some ways a culmination of many years' experience, and many supportive professional colleagues, along with a recognition by Northern Trust of my skill set. The position was a good fit for me, the salary was excellent, and I was working with people who respected and listened to my advice. This did not mean that work life was easy. It was however rewarding. I was able to hire good people, secretaries, and professional consultants. I was truly able to create the EAP department as I thought it should be. I was also able to advocate for better mental health care as a part of the employee benefits push of the mid 1990's. In my final years, the Family Assistance Program I was able to expand the program into Mental Health Disability management, an area new at the time to the EAP field. This meant a lot of internal corporate negotiations and a few power and control conflicts which were challenging but worthy corporate battles waged with integrity. This was, for me a professional climax and I was becoming ready to retire while on a high.

During my nine years at Northern Trust, there were a few notable moments. In addition to the core services of assessment or diagnosis, referral to appropriate treatment resources, and follow-up or after-care for Northern

Trust employees and family members, the Family Assistance Program was a part of Northern's essential services in times of crisis. Critical Incident Management and Crisis Intervention were provided when, in 1992, Hurricane Andrew hit Miami and Northern Trust's Miami office on Brickell Avenue. The damage to the physical structure by the category five hurricane was extensive. The role of the Family Assistance Program was to work with the many employees and family members impacted by the storm. Beyond physical damage and inconveniences there were traumatized people, and complicated family systems to assist in a return to normal. I spent some time on site but the primary asset for employees was the local provider of Family Assistance Program services. A complicating factor in this recovery effort was that the local Family Assistance provider and his family were themselves victims of the hurricane. A team effort of our Miami Family Assistance provider and our clinical backup from Fort Lauderdale worked with senior bank management to assist in the recovery. As trying as the work was, it formed a great bond of management and Family Assistance Program.

In 1993, Northern Trust's New York offices, housed in the World Trade Center were just one of many offices affected by the first bombing of the World Trade Center towers. I had been to the site several times prior to the bombing, which took place in the parking ramp under the Trade Center. So, when I returned after the bombing, I myself had that strange otherworldly visual of the devastation in and around the complex. Previously established contacts and a network of crisis services were called into action. A team met with nearly all employees to assess their needs and their ability to return to work under combat zone conditions. There was a need to work with both the people who worked at World Trade Center, now displaced, and the nearest Northern Trust office on Broad Street since for the moment, all work would be condensed into the Broad Street Office. The increased tensions and anxieties placed a strain on the workplace and often exacerbated home-based problems.

One area of influence I was proud of in my work with the corporation, was advocacy in the area of Human Resources for better mental health and substance abuse benefits. Often this took on an adversarial tone with the corporation's selected health insurance providers. What looked like favorable pricing on a corporate level often included some shaving of benefits in the area of mental health and substance abuse by the contracted insurance providers. These were always tough meetings but I was pleased with corporate support and the results. This same advocacy on the employee's behalf was later extended to mental health disabilities. In my last two years at Northern Trust, I successfully promoted the Family Assistance Program as the manager of mental health disabilities and the primary interface with the insurance providers in that area. Frankly, this was most difficult work. I am not certain that the

FAP had any better outcomes in terms of length of the disabilities — our internal studies showed only a modest difference in the length of disabilities when compared to other companies and insurances. But I do know that the employees had qualitative differences in better access to care during their disabilities and the tone of advocacy on behalf of the employee. These were unexpected collateral benefits for the corporation.

But "all work and no play make Jack a dull boy," as the saying goes. For both Linda and me, our professional lives were very demanding, yet rewarding both personally and financially. We had friends who were equally as stretched in their work lives and when we found time to be together it was always a treat. For the last ten years of our life in Chicago we had two glamorous evenings each year which we shared with our friends as combined social events and fundraisers for Episcopal Charities. These were held sometime after Thanksgiving around the feast of St Nicholas and a second similar fundraiser for the cathedral around the date of the Epiphany. Both events were held at Chicago's old and glorious Drake Hotel. These were black tie evenings with fine dining and dancing. We enjoyed home entertaining usually in a bit of an upscale setting using our collected treasures of silver and family heirlooms. We treated ourselves to Chicago's theatre, not often enough, to the symphony and the Lyric Opera. Much of this was a world, in a galaxy far away, from that which Linda's or my family would have chosen or envisioned for us. It was also a life that we ourselves, in our teens would not have ever seen written in our stars. And our journey to this place, well, ... it was uncharted. But this was our life in Chicago with our adopted family and friends grown from beginnings, and over twenty plus years of love and care.

"Look up at the stars, not at your feet. Try to make sense of what you see, and wonder what makes the universe exist. Be Curious."
— Stephen Hawking

All of the above did not happen by chance. Early on in our married life we used each New Year's Eve as an annual financial review and goal setting time. Neither of us were likely to "ring out the old and ring in the new" with partying of the "Times Square" variety. We preferred to be at home or perhaps at the theater with a quiet dinner after theater. Initially, our New Year's celebrations were very modest, of financial necessity. As the years progressed, our celebrations grew more elegant as we made ourselves "tourists" in some of the fine hotels and restaurants of our home city of Chicago. But each year the agenda was the same. We made a financial review of the year past, set financial goals for the new year, and set individual and joint personal goals. This is a tradition that we have kept for 40 plus years of marriage. These annual "retreats" were for more than just financial accounting. It was during these annual New Year's goal setting celebrations that we first made our plans for research vacations for a future life in France and for our retirement.

Somewhere around the late 1980's we realized that, given our career choices, it was unlikely that a traditional corporate sponsored retirement plan would be ours. We were alternating between self-employment, and occasional periods of employment by corporations. We set up a Self-Employment Pension Plan (SEP) and met with a Certified Financial Planner. Each year we set our financial goals and met them with the same commitment and seriousness as we met our personal and professional goals. We intentionally maxed-out both pre- and post-tax investment options each year. Originally, we set our retirement age at sixty. But as our work life became more and more demanding and the 1990's return on investment bubble grew bigger and bigger, an earlier retirement became more appealing and ever more possible.

"There was nowhere to go but everywhere, so just keep on rolling under the stars"
— Jack Kerouac – 1922 – 1969 French-Canadian, American novelist, and poet

For our celebration of the Millennium New Year we decided to avoid the all the special deals attracting New Year's revelers and for a change offered to celebrate this new year with our closest friends at home. Our lovely restored 1880's Queen Anne Victorian had served us well not only as our home but also as our entry into the B&B hospitality business (a part-time adventure on top of our full-time professional careers). For this New Year we would host our personal guests overnight and avoid the crowds downtown. We provided special champagne flute souvenirs and chocolates and everyone contributed to a tastefully extravagant evening of dinner and dancing at home. As it turned out it was a glorious way to begin the new millennium and set us on our way to France for our retirement.

The year 2000 was for us, a year of saying goodbye to our home. We put it on the market, an offer was made, and it closed February 2001. We said a gradual goodbye to our careers, I left my position at Northern Trust in February 2001. And a grand hello to our new adventure in France.

"He was there alone with himself, collected, tranquil, adoring,
comparing the serenity of his heart with the serenity of the skies,
moved in the darkness by the visible splendors of the constellations,
and the invisible splendor of God, opening his soul to the thoughts
which fall from the Unknown.

In such moments, offering up his heart at the hour when the flowers of night
breathed their perfume, lighted like a lamp in the center of the starry night,
expanding his soul in ecstasy in the midst of the universal radiance of creation,
he could not himself perhaps have told what was passing in his own mind;
he felt something depart from him, and something descend upon him,
mysterious interchanges of the depths of the soul with the depths of the universe."
— Victor Hugo, *Les Misérables*

Notes from Chicago, Love and Care Years

[1] **Erik Erikson** in a nutshell, identifies the age of 20-39 with the human task of resolving our need for intimacy vs. isolation, which becomes prominent around the age of 30. Once people have established their identities, they are ready to make long-term commitments to others. They become capable of forming intimate, reciprocal relationships (e.g. through close friendships or marriage) and willingly make the sacrifices and compromises that such relationships require. In middle adulthood, ages 40 -59, the primary developmental task is one of contributing to society and helping to guide future generations vs. personal stagnation. When a person contributes during this period, perhaps by raising a family or working toward the betterment of society, a sense of generativity—a sense of productivity and accomplishment—results.

[2] In total, over time, we purchased two condominiums, and three houses. Each one became a home in which we put our creative mark on them. Initially this was done instinctively, but after observations and comments from many people, including B&B guests and prospective buyers at the time of sale, our home-making became a more conscious effort to create visually appealing, sensually soothing, and spiritually inspiring living spaces. The story of the renovation of our French ruin is told in *Bright Sun & Long Shadows* available at Parsons Porch Books (parsonsporch.com/episcopal-books) and Amazon.com (Trafford Press).

[3] **Zebra** is the American medical slang for arriving at an exotic medical diagnosis when a more commonplace explanation is more likely. It is shorthand for the aphorism coined in the late 1940s by Theodore Woodward, professor at the University of Maryland School of Medicine, who instructed his medical interns: "When you hear hoofbeats, think of horses not zebras." Since horses are common in Maryland while zebras are relatively rare, logically one could confidently guess that an animal making hoofbeats is probably a horse. By 1960, the aphorism was widely known in medical circles. The modified version used above is from Harley S. Smyth

[4] **Bi-vocational Clergy** is a term used in the church to describe clergy who earn their living in some area of secular work, and as clergy offer their services to the church, sometimes paid by the church, sometime not paid, but as a gift to the church. As noted earlier in this book, I worked for seven years on the Bishop's staff as paid diocesan clergy. In time I would change to accept positions in the corporate world in the field of Employee Assistance Programs. While working full time in corporate America, I offered my services to the diocese as Assisting Clergy at the Cathedral, and as occasional Interim Clergy

in parishes in transition, and also as a consultant for the diocese to parishes in trouble. Bi-vocational clergy are also sometimes referred to as "tentmakers" with reference to St Paul who according to tradition was a tentmaker and apostle to the gentile congregations in Antioch, Corinth, Ephesus, and others noted in the New Testament Epistles.

[5] At the time, in the late 1980's, Arthur Andersen & Co was among the world's top five accounting firms. Andersen Accounting and their consulting services were parts of the same corporation. After the 1990's, the consulting offices split from accounting to become Accenture, and the accounting side of Arthur Andersen & Co would become a casualty of the Enron scandal of 2001. But at the time. In the late 1980's this was a plum EAP contract.

[6] In the corporate jargon of today "To Make the Elephant Dance" has taken on a more positive nuance — refer to the 2015 book, *Making the Elephant Dance* by Ratan N. Tata. The phrase would eventually mean a skillful series of growth initiatives designed to transplant best practices from one company to another to grow from local excellence to a global powerhouse. But, 25 years earlier, in the early 1990s, and in the hands of relatively inexperienced new management, "Making the Elephant Dance," simply meant "it's my way, or the highway." In the 2020s, the Elephant is where your organization is today. There are phases of change between traditional environments and modern environments. Some organizations have the luxury to start from scratch, but for many, the challenge is teaching their lumbering elephant to dance like a nimble ballerina. My experience of this phrase in the 1990s was more like the African parable quoted in the text, "When the Elephant Dances the Mouse May Die."

An Epilogue

Life does not have to be perfect to be wonderful. The steps toward maturity, it seems, are always and necessarily immature. What else could they be?
–Richard Rohr, *The Universal Christ*

Well, gentle reader, if you have made it this far, you know that this is only the end of the book not the end of the story. At this point, you have followed my life for 53 years. Both Linda and I will be stepping out on a new adventure. While this book is the third book written, this account of the early years is a prequel to our retirement years recounted in *Bright Sun & Long Shadows*, and *Le Petit Jardin de L'âme* which tell of our twelve years of retirement living in France. Perhaps someday I will continue the story to include our life in the Republic of Panama from 2012 onward. I have enjoyed sharing these stories with you, thank you for coming on this journey with me.

I have just two more anecdotes and a few observations about *Constellations at Twilight* before I say good-bye. The tales below mix past and present experiences in a way which might encourage you to search your own biography for events that replay themselves in your present life.

You may remember, at the beginning of my story how I was aware early on that I was "out-of-sync" with family expectations, particularly my father. This quality lingered on, lifelong, through many years. We did learn to live with it and learned to laugh at it from time to time and perhaps to love it. But it was forever there. One time when Linda and I were living in France, my family came to visit. It was my parents' second visit and my brother and sister-in-law's first visit. They expressed their interest in visiting parts of France that we had already visited a few times and were not interested in going back. I also knew that after a week or so together, we would appreciate a rest from each other. So, I mapped out a five-day journey to the areas they wanted to see. I made the B&B and hotel reservations and after a few days of coaching, sent them on their way. For starters, and not quite according to plan, they encountered an unexpected and serious fire which caused a detour to their first night's destination. But they arrived at the town, checked in, and discovered, that because of the fire, there was no power. That meant no air conditioning in the room and rather limited dinner options. Fortunately, my family made the best of the situation. The next day they travelled to explore Monaco as they had hoped. All went well for the days in Monaco. On their return trip, I routed them to one of France's many "most beautiful villages." I had selected rooms inside the old walls of a mountain-top fortress-village. Linda and I had been there once before and thought it would be a delightful taste of France they would not forget. As they were driving along the road, not yet ascending to the mountain top, my father looked up to see the village, perched precariously on high, and according to my brother, said "Who in their right mind would go up there?," to which my brother responded, "That's where Val is sending us!" I believe that they enjoyed the excursion, but it was a forever reminder of how out-of-sync we still were.

"Perhaps they are not stars in the sky.
But rather openings where our loved ones
shine down to let us know they are happy."
— attributed to Charlie Brown, Charles Schulz

Linda and I have our "out-of-sync" moments; during forty-plus years of marriage there are bound to be a few. But for the most part, I have found a partner which whom I am well attuned on most things. And for some others we have learned, sometimes with great effort, to dance to the same music. In our Chicago lives we tried our hand at ballroom dance classes, twice. As it turns out, this was a highly symbolic exercise. The first attempt nearly ended in divorce. But we tried it again and were happy with our progress. During this second attempt we managed to get a few dance variations under our belt and even took ourselves on some ballroom dance Sunday afternoons with classic big bands and spacious dance floors. We particularly enjoyed the tango. We would never be contestants on *Dancing with the Stars* but we were reasonably confident and comfortable to enjoy dancing. One evening, during one of the annual dinner dance fundraisers for the diocese, well into the evening, the band started up with a tango. The dance floor thinned out a bit and we saw it as our opportunity to have more room to dance with just a few brave couples on the floor. We danced, and we enjoyed ourselves. As the tango played on, we lost ourselves in the dance. When the music stopped, we looked around to find that we were indeed the ONLY couple on the dance floor! We smiled, a little blush came to our cheeks, we returned to our table with an approving hum running through the room and a cherished memory in our hearts.

Being out-of-sync with my family of origin was initially disturbing to me. In turn, such incongruities provided a rationale for sometimes painful differences. But in the end, in love, and with a bit of laughter, such variance was just the way it was. At other times being aware that one is out-of-step can be a first step in learning a new dance in life. But the life lesson is; either way, each can have its own joy.

"More than half the stars in the universe
are orphan-stars belonging to no constellation.
And they give off more light than all the constellation stars."
—John Peter Berger, 1926-2017 — *Confabulations*

For as long as I can remember, I have always been curious, always been searching, and very much aware of being on a journey to somewhere. I have also been frustrated in that journey, at times impatient, at times depressed. In the re-telling of my life, I see that some things appear to remain constant, but in fact, they do change, even if imperceptibly. Yes, the earth wobbles on its axis, stars are born and die and seem to streak through the galaxy. Indeed, even the night sky, and the stars have individual differences and universal constants. In all, the cosmos just keeps on, getting on, and we too find our way. Know that we are now exactly where we are supposed to be, and we will be where we are meant to be. Perhaps our task is not to get anywhere, but rather to make the most of where we are. To be completely, purely, in the present moment may be the way to see our way to the future.

Lead, Kindly Light, amid the encircling gloom, Lead Thou me on! The night is dark, and I am far from home, Lead Thou me on! Keep Thou my feet: I do not ask to see the distant scene,—one step enough for me. — John Henry Newman, *1833* - written as a poem "The Pillar of the Cloud", most often sung to the hymn-tune *Sandon*.

And it seems that after years and years on a path of discipline, of self-control, of academics and education, I have had to unlearn, and relearn. There is more to life than the planned, ordered, and rational. The spontaneous and intuitive, inspiration of visionaries and seers are not antitheses, rather, they are complementary aspects of becoming more fully human. There is a harmony. Too often, importance is placed on one view over the other. Seeing the world differently, is not better than, but is a glimpse of the creator's infinite variety. What we know, and what we may see, could be a starry pinpoint in the night sky. Or is it? Could the stars at twilight be some greater light from yet another dimension, merely veiled by our everyday dusks and dawns? Heads-up! Look beyond Constellations at Twilight.

Annotated Bibliography

Bly, Robert. *Iron John: A Book about Men*. Boston: Da Capo Press, a member of the Perseus group. ©1990, 2004 Robert Bly - Although not directly quoted in my writing, I found Bly's book an incentive to write my story with the tone and with the personal anecdotes that I chose.

Cilliers, J.H. *Mysterium tremendum et fascinans: Liturgical Perspectives on the Approach to God* Department of Practical Theology & Missiology University of Stellenbosch STELLENBOSCH. ©2009 – This more contemporary paper begins with Rudolf Otto's 1917 work, *Das Heilige* (The Sacred) Otto's theories underline the fact that our experiences of the Holy are complex and not to be taken too lightly. His contribution to this discussion is important, because he somehow succeeded in combining both the realities of the so-called subjective side of religion, incorporating, on the one hand, all the existential components of humanity, and on the other, also the reality of the revelation of God. We approach God because God approaches us. The concepts in Otto's work, along with Mircea Eliade's work, were both life-time gifts from Seminary Education.

Eliade, Mircea. *The Sacred and the Profane:* The nature of Religion, The significance of Religious myth and Symbolism and ritual within life and culture. Translated from the French by Willard R. Trask. A Harvest Book, Harcourt, Brace & World Inc ©1957 Rowohlt Taschenbuch Verlag GmbH, ©1959 English, by Harcourt, ©1987 renewed by Harcourt. Eliade shows that sacred space is understood as a place where the eternal meets the temporal, where the divine dwells with the human. This book is fundamental and foundational to much of my thinking before my writings and is no doubt reflected in my outlook. Truly a gift of my seminary education.

Maynard, Dennis R. *When Sheep Attack*, Published by Booksurge Publishers ©2010 Dennis R. Maynard D.Min. This book features prominently in the congregational conflict recounted in my book *Le Petit Jardin de L'âme*. My work with congregations in conflict mentioned in *Constellations at Twilight* precedes Maynard's study and his book. But the congregation I refer to could well have been a case study for Maynard's book.

Reiter, Leo J. *I am an Ex-Marine*, Independently Published, November 2018. A different personal journey from my own but in addition to providing some humor about those teen years at Prep Seminary, it reflects another man's interior journey and life choices.

www.ingramcontent.com/pod-product-compliance
Lightning Source LLC
Chambersburg PA
CBHW052110110526
44592CB00013B/1550